THE JOY OF VOLUNTEERING

working & surviving in developing countries...

by

Othniel J. Seiden, MD

founder of Doctors to the World

Cover Art
by Capri Brock

Proudly Published in the USA

www.BooomerBookSeries.com

ISBN: 1519495587

DEDICATED TO

Mathew Potter

world traveler, teacher, law student….

Table of Contents

PURPOSE

Over these past decades, I've had the pleasure and the privilege of serving on several volunteer medical missions throughout the Third world, developing countries, underprivileged areas in the US and abroad as well as disaster zones of our planet. Though these adventures have been completely on a volunteer basis, their rewards have been great and varied. Upon returning from each of these experiences, **I've always been asked by others, "How can I get involved with such a mission?"** It forever surprises me that in spite of the fact that the need for volunteers is immense, information on how to go about getting involved isn't that easy to come by. That is the purpose of writing this guidebook.

The intent is for this book to be more than just a listing of organizations who will be delighted to have your help and get you out into the disadvantaged and more primitive areas of the world. As I review my experiences over the past years, I realize there is much I now take for granted, things that I know now because of sometimes painful trial-and-error and hard knocks.

Knowing these "things" beforehand would have made my life as a volunteer infinitely easier. I hope to impart this knowledge, learned through my trial-and-error, to you in hopes of making your adventures more enjoyable and the volunteer experience more efficient, effective and rewarding.

There are hundreds of organizations sending selfless volunteers out to do good work for those who are less fortunate. Most of those organizations have neither the personnel nor the funds to adequately prepare their volunteers to properly cope with the strange environs they will encounter when leaving the culture they have been used to.

It's truly a different world out there, and the better you prepare for it the better off you and those you're trying to help will be.

Don't let the fact that I work in the field of health care fool you into thinking volunteerism or this manual is only for physicians, dentists and nurses. **The underprivileged areas of the world need educators, agriculturist, technicians of all types, administrators, builders, plumbers, craftsmen, skilled and knowledgeable people in <u>every</u> walk of life.**

This book should be helpful to you in whatever field your expertise and talents lie. Most of the problems encountered in primitive parts of the world or in disaster areas will effect anyone from our culture in much the same way. Preventing "<u>culture shock</u>" is the same problem for all of us, whether we are physician, merchant or chief thief. Prevention or reduction of culture shock, enabling us to perform most efficiently, is the real purpose and crux of this guide.

In addition to volunteer missions, more and more American corporations are sending personnel into the Third World to open offices, factories and to represent them in new markets.

These employees will face many of the same problems that volunteers face, though their living conditions often, but not always, may be somewhat better. Thus, this manual and what it teaches will be just as important and useful to those paid individuals as they face their foreign cultures.

Chapter 1

The Joy of Volunteering

I'm sure there are as many reasons for volunteering, to go "out in the bush" to give of yourself, as there are people providing services. To some, it's a way of "giving back," or repaying for the blessings we have of the "good life" here in our culture. To others it's a pure "lust for adventure." Maybe you're just "looking for a change." "It's a way to keep up skills," if you're retired or semi-retired. "A way to keep my hands in." "It's a terrific way to see the world." "It gets me out of my specialty for a little while and lets me do some real grass roots down to earth work." It's something I like to do once a year to get my own life back on track, to get me out of the rut and help me put everything back in proper perspective." "It lets me reevaluate my priorities, reestablish my value system, aim for my goals in life!"

These are just a few of the answers I've gotten from others who volunteer for missions in underdeveloped areas of this planet.

For most of us, several of the above reasons go into our decisions to keep going back for more.

Each of us has other reasons of our own for doing this type of work. Volunteerism is a "right thing to do" and there really "aren't too many wrong reasons for doing it."

Whatever your reasons are for pursuing involvement in this type of effort, you'll discover many additional reasons before you're through. It <u>is</u> adventure! It <u>is</u> satisfying! You <u>do</u> contribute a great deal of needed skill and service! You <u>do</u> make an impact, leave your mark! You <u>do</u> feel better about yourself when you're finished! And you'll discover you learn much more than you teach, and take away with you more than you can possibly give!

All the above and much more make up *"The Joy of Volunteering."*

If you're interested in traveling the world as a volunteer, the following chapters will tell you how to get involved. They will point out some of the hardships, how to prepare for them, how to avoid the avoidable ones, and how to handle those you can't dodge.

I hope this guidebook will paint as accurate a picture as possible. What some call inconveniences and difficult situations, others will look upon as adventures. The very things that turn some of you on to volunteerism will turn others off, and that's O.K. Volunteerism isn't for everyone. If it's not for you, find it out now in this manual, not out in the field where it will make you miserable and disappoint those depending on you. Learn how to pick assignments more compatible with your liking. There is no point in going out into a situation where you'll have trouble functioning. There are others who will find conditions in such places challenging and exciting. If primitive isn't your cup of tea, look for another location, less primitive, with less language problems, more developed, less culturally different and more fitting to your interests.

There are a wide variety of assignments in all parts of the world, many here in the United States, all important projects and several that will fit your desires. <u>Don't feel you have to pick the toughest your first time out!</u>

If you have a Caribbean type personality, pick an island with beaches and sunshine; if you thrive on adventure look at Africa, Central America, South America, India or any one of the more primitive or exciting places you've always been curious to see. Don't want to get too far from home? Go to one of the American Indian reservations or work with migrant farmers in our Southwestern states. You can get assignments in the Southeastern states as well, or in the Northeast, Northwest or Midwest. You don't even have to leave home to volunteer! President Jimmy Carter's favorite charity, *Habitat for Humanity* builds homes in virtually every State in the Union and uses volunteers from every walk of life and nearly all ages.

This manual should warn you about the possible hardships, so they can be avoided by a little research on your part, and help you thoughtfully select a location fitting your personality. **If you will be accompanied by family, consider them, too.**

So read on and learn as much about volunteerism as you can before you make up your mind. There are places where your skills are needed. Try to get together and learn first hand the ***Joy of Volunteering.***

CHAPTER 2

FINDING YOUR ASSIGNMENT

There are thousands of organizations whose major activity is getting personnel and needy locations together. They span the continuum from small church or synagogue *social action committees*, to organizations like the Peace Corp.

Perhaps the best place for you to start your quest is locally through churches, schools, YMCAs, civic groups, libraries, the local Red Cross chapter, Salvation Army, American Heart Association, American Cancer Society, the local March of Dimes chapter, the American Lung Association, hospital auxiliary, Boy Scouts, Girl Scouts, etc., etc., etc.

These organizations can give you a taste of the satisfaction you can gain from volunteering with little risk on your part.

You can get a taste of the "Joy" without having to venture far from home, committing weeks, month or years of your life or giving up much time from work or leisure.

If you want to start off in a worldlier manner, there are hundreds of organizations ready to help you there, too. Your first step is to contact them and get on their mailing lists. They will send you indexes of their assignments periodically, or notify you when posts become available in which you might have an interest. Just drop them a post card, letter, or as I prefer, give them a call. An enormous resource for you is no further than your computer and the Internet.

Just search on "Volunteer Organizations" and you will find it's easy to get on their e-mail lists, or to request information.

That way you can find out a little more about one another, right at the outset. In the Appendix of this manual are listed a number of organizations who could use your help. The list is far from complete, but it provides a representative cross section of organizations. There are many more out there trying to do equally important work.

If you don't find one to fit your needs, do some research on your own. Check with local churches for leads to missions of a religious type. Go to your local library for listings of other groups, perhaps of a more secular nature. Check with the US Government

Printing Office nearest you. Investigate through your local media, which often is called upon by regional, national and international groups to give them help in recruitment and fund raising. If you are serious about giving of yourself, the excuse, "I couldn't find a place to provide service," just won't fly. If in the end you really can't find an organization that fills the niche you want to work in, then do what other specifically committed people do every day all over the world; start an organization of your own that precisely addresses your area of interest.

Even a small group of committed people working in concert can make a tremendous impact locally, nationally and internationally.

Realize that almost every organization out there, even the huge ones, started off with just one or two inspired and dedicated individuals no different than you.

However, before you start your own organization check the listing of existing groups in the Appendix of this handbook. There are probably several addressing the problems you are interested in helping to solve. That doesn't mean that there isn't room for another group that can do the job better, in a different way, or just helping to accomplish a common goal. But, the easiest way to reach your purpose may be through serving with an existing association. Why "reinvent the wheel" if good ones are already rolling?

If the above suggestions don't find you a place to

start then by all means do give some serious thought to starting an organization of your own. There is an outline of how to do just that in Chapter 13 of this manual.

CHAPTER 3

PREPARATIONS

CULTURE SHOCK!!!!

Your plane has just landed on a runway in a remote Central American city. Because of missed connections along the way, through no fault of yours, you are arriving a day late. Not unusual when traveling Puddle Jumper Airline, the only one serving this area. You've not been able to phone ahead to let your "welcoming committee" know of your new schedule because once outside of the USA, communications "just ain't like home!" Unless you got a special cell phone, yours hasn't worked since you took off in the good old USA. Still, you are anticipating a warm welcome from the locals. After all, they know you're coming. Surely they realize you've missed connections and can figure out you'll be on a later plane. After all, this is a rather fine thing you're doing ... to come to this remote place on our globe to give your time and talent to help these underprivileged people.

The ancient DC-3, vintage 1937, the only way into this place, finally bounces to a stop on the dirt runway, and the pilot (there is no stewardess) points to the door, letting you know it's time to get out.

Wrestling your luggage from the plane to the airport makes you appreciate what airline personnel have been doing for you for years. Finally inside the terminal, you realize customs is giving you no breaks even if you are coming to give of yourself. When you finally get to repack, you realize you've got more of a language problem than you thought you would. Their English, though much better than your Spanish, leaves much to be desired.

CULTURE SHOCK!!!!

Coming out of customs you realize your reception committee hasn't shown up yet, or again, or if it ever will. It seems the only interest in you is by a dozen urchins who surround you noisily. Half are begging, and the other half are fighting to carry your luggage for tips.

CULTURE SHOCK!!!!

At last, a taxi driver approaches you. He speaks passing English and you are able to make yourself partly understood. He tells you he knows a nice place where you can have a room and meals. He'll take you there and then try to make contact with your "reception committee" and get you together with them.

It's a good idea and you agree; anything to get away from these "helpful" kids. Anyway he seems your only hope right now.

You're delivered to your "no star" accommodations

in his 1957 Oldsmobile. His sister checks you in.

He leads you to your room and shows you where to fill your wash bowl in case you'd like to freshen up a bit. He also points to where you can empty your bladder, etc., if are you so inclined.

He leaves for the airport and you crash on the bed. It's hard as a rock except for where it sags in the middle like a sway back nag. The sheets are clean though and you're truly thankful for that. You hear yourself saying, "Dear God, what am I doing here?" If you're still an optimist you might be saying, "This too shall pass!"

You're experiencing *"CULTURE SHOCK!!!!"*

Mercifully, you fall asleep from sheer exhaustion. You sleep through the dinner that comes with your room, but you won't mind when you discover later the entree was Guinea Pig, the local specialty.

A shy and gentle knock on your door awakens you.

Miracles do happen! The cabby did find your people. They had met every plane after the one you missed, except the one you were on. He found them at the airport waiting for the next one you could have been on. "It's the thought that counts!" you tell yourself.

Their English is no better than the cabby's, but thanks to heaven, it's no worse. They apologize up and down and make you feel a lot better about your decision to have come to help. They tell you that they will pick you up in the morning and take you on the next leg of your journey to the village where you'll be working. You are to be ready at 8:00 a.m., which will give you plenty of time for a good night's sleep and breakfast.

You feel much better having made contact with your people and begin to note the pangs of your missed dinner. The cabby's sister offers you some fruit. It's fantastic. This is fruit country, after all. Things are looking up a bit. But you're still exhausted and go back to your room to sleep --- into more of a coma, actually.

Morning comes.

You haven't moved a muscle all night. You can't remember ever having slept so soundly. You're refreshed and the world looks much better than the night before.

You wait your turn to use the toilet. Then you bathe as best you can out of the wash bowl and pitcher in your room. The room doesn't look any better to you this morning than it did last night. But today you move on so it doesn't really matter. After all, you did come for some adventure ... to experience how others live.

Breakfast is the strongest coffee you've ever tasted (even though it's 70% milk), bread and cheese and more of that wonderful fruit.

Breakfast finished you wait for your companions.

And wait ... and wait....

Nine a.m. comes and passes.

Ten.

Eleven.

You don't know were to go to find them. Do you dare leave to look for them?

Eleven fifteen! Damned inconsiderate!

Eleven twenty. What a waste of your time!

Eleven twenty-five!

"Why did I let myself in for this?"

CULTURE SHOCK!!!!

Eleven thirty and they finally show up, in a truck about a decade older than the cab that brought you from the airport. They apologize for being late, but you don't fully understand their reason, which has something to do with the vehicle. Oh well, "all's well that ends well."

You bounce off, three of you crowded in the narrow truck cab. At least two of you didn't use deodorant this morning! The ride is slow, bouncy, hot, dusty and you understand only a smattering of what they are saying to you.

"Dear God, what am I doing here?" you mumble to yourself again. This time you wonder if, "This too will pass!"

Four hours later you pull into a remote jungle village. It's hot! It's humid! It's primitive! It's oppressive!

CULTURE SHOCK!!!!

You find your self mumbling, "Why me?"

The truck stops by a straw hut on stilts.

This is your home and clinic!" they proudly inform you. You find yourself wishing you were back in the "no star hotel" from last night. Would it be possible to commute? It's only a fleeting thought.

This is CULTURE SHOCK!!!!

Roaches. Lizards. Bedbugs ---

CULTURE SHOCK!

Don't despair; everyone experiences some degree of culture shock.

It can't be totally avoided. The trick is to minimize it and turn it into an adventure. It's almost a matter of attitude control, and it begins long before you leave the familiar comforts of your home. The more surprises you can anticipate, or eliminate, the less shock you'll suffer.

Of course, no one can anticipate every near disaster. But most of the experiences in the above scenario weren't anywhere near disasters. The above story is a bit extreme, but that's because it is a composite of several experiences I've had on several missions. Each mission had but one and at most two such "culture shocks." Some of you read it wondering, "Why would I ever let myself in for that kind of experience?" It may surprise you that just as many or more read that and thought, "What a fun adventure that would be!" or **"That's the kind of adventure that would be worth going on just for the great stories I could tell for the rest of my life!"**

The fact is that if you are forewarned about such surprises, they become very tolerable. And if they are not for you, then the forewarning will let you seek out a more compatible mission for yourself, perhaps one where you could go with a group to a less primitive and foreign culture.

And there is no reason to apologize if the more primitive places are not for you. Need exists everywhere and the good you can do anywhere makes the world a better place for all of us.

Most of us could cope with any three or four of those situations with little effort. And after a short while you'll be laughing them off, "Ha ha, that wasn't really so bad, and it really did pass." It's only when you are overwhelmed by so many surprises at once that you feel you're facing impending doom. So, the second defense against culture shock is to put everything into perspective and prioritize and solve only one disaster at a time, the most overwhelming first.

Memorize the following truism, for when all else fails, this will pull you through. Say to yourself, over and over again, *"This too shall pass!"*

Let's go through these three steps one at time.

Preparation:

Here I'm talking about preparation psychologically as well as physically, which may lead you to make some material provisions also.

As soon as you find out your destination, immerse yourself in learning everything you can about the area. Unfortunately, with many Third World countries this might be more difficult than you think. Most places you might be going to aren't along the "beaten paths" or tourist spots. Very little may be written about these places, and what's been committed to ink and paper may be obscure and hard to find. Never-the-less, start by calling your travel agent. He or she probably won't have much information about the specific place, but ask anyway. She may have valuable material about the continent, country, district, etc. Every little bit helps. Then turn to the encyclopedia. If one doesn't have anything, then try another. Different encyclopedias vary greatly in their coverage of subjects.

National Geographic Magazine may have something on your destination. It has been published since 1896 and is fully indexed. Try your main library. If the latest thing published about the place happens to be in an issue from way back, look it up anyway. Remember, things don't usually change too much in the Third World. That's partly why they are Third World. Try to find out everything you can about the place, its history, economy, government, weather, living conditions, foods, lifestyles, clothing, animals, insects, communications, languages, education system, religions ... and above all, its people.

The more you know the less you'll be surprised. Even bedbugs and roaches aren't the threat you expect them to be if you know something about them before your first encounter. Taking the right bug repellent can make a gigantic difference.

Don't just learn about the major cities. More than likely you will be going into the back country, and life there may be quite different. I was recently in Ecuador for a three week tour of duty. Most of what I read about the country dealt with conditions in Quito and Guayaquil, two lovely and modern cities. You couldn't imagine a nicer place to travel and visit, with all the modern conveniences of home. But the village where we were stationed, Guaranda, was quite another matter. It was 90 miles South of Quito at about 10,000 feet altitude in the Andean Mountains. In Quito most people speak some English; in Guaranda virtually no one does. In fact, the Indians there speak a Spanish dialect much their own, so you might have some language problems even if proficient in Spanish. Guaranda is to Quito as the Missouri Ozarks are to New York City. There's nothing wrong with the Missouri Ozarks, they are beautiful, but if you were coming from Quito and had read up on New York City, you'd be somewhat surprised at what you'd find in the Ozarks.

In Quito you can survive on credit cards as in any tourist economy. However, in Guaranda I discovered credit cards were worthless, though today that might be different. You'll need more cash in non-tourist economies even for such necessities as room and food if they are not picked up for you by the host country or organization sending you. Be forewarned, it can be disastrous being merely penniless in a foreign country.

Ecuador being on the equator makes most people think it will be hot there. I did my tour of duty during July and August. Hot? At 10,000 feet altitude it never got warmer than 64 degrees in the day and dropped to 40 degrees Fahrenheit at night. The only thing we had in common with the tropics was palm trees which were growing at 10,000 feet in the mountains ... a very strange sight indeed.

Many Third World destinations have very unstable governments, and though your work will most likely be apolitical and you, if you're smart, will avoid talk about anything political, it would be wise to know what is going on, especially what they think of Americans. Also, let our embassy know where you'll be and what you're supposed to be doing. It could help protect you and save them some embarrassment if any questions about you and your project were directed toward them. A brief note with your itinerary and job description is all it takes. Furthermore, get a letter of introduction from the organization sending you stating why you are there. Get it on official letterhead. If you can also get one from the embassy it will be very helpful. Official looking paper with signatures can get you through lots of doors even if they don't know what's written on it. It is also worth trying to get some official papers from the host government you are visiting. If you are going to do good work for them, the local politicians love to take credit and will usually happily cooperate.

The best source of information about the place and project should be available from the organization sending you in. If they can't answer pertinent questions for you, think twice about their credibility. To me that means they have not done their research and you may be no more than the fool their sending out to test the waters. If the organization is legitimate, and most are, they should be able to answer most of your questions and give you the names and phone numbers of your predecessors who should be willing to give you an honest report of their experiences.

I am medical director for the organizations ***Doctors To The World, Dentists For The World, Volunteers To The World*** and ***Student Volunteers To The World.*** We will not send anyone out into any area that I, or one of our officers, have not personally visited. All of our programs and projects, with the exception of natural disasters which require instant response, are planned and set up during on site visits. We purposely check out the living and working accommodations, needs, food supplies, water supplies, as well as political situations, needs of the areas, hazards and attractions of interest. We encourage our new volunteers heading to an area to contact those who have been there before to get as many opinions as possible. Any organization sending you out into the field owes you no less. Most will be as helpful. They know that it is vital for you to go in with your eyes open. That is what will help you avoid *culture shock* and it is culture shock which can make you impotent to do your best work.

Prioritizing:

When, in spite of all your planning and preparing yourself, all still seems to go wrong at once (and there will be such times) don't punt; *prioritize*.

Triage the situation, and solve your most desperate situation first.

Find a person you can communicate with and who can translate for you if necessary. Aloneness in a foreign place can be devastating. Finding anyone with whom you can converse is a tremendous help. Then, solve as many of your problems as you can, one at a time. Be flexible. If you find conditions such that you can't perform the exact task you were sent there for, go to plan B, which you may have to invent right then and there. Determine what the next most essential needs are and forget the originals.

If you can communicate with the outside world, try to reach the organization that sent you in and discuss your situation. If you can't find a telephone, look for the next best thing. I was once incommunicado in Zona Miskito, Honduras for over two weeks because there were no phones, until I found a missionary with a short wave radio. He reached a ham radio operator in Florida who got my message home. This poor of communication is rare, but it does exist. If conditions are that primitive your organization should know about it and discuss contingency plans before you go.

An interesting phenomenon has occurred in the past few years. FAX has reached the Third World. It amazes me that even some of the most primitive areas seem to have FAX machines. The most humorous Fax situation was when I was in Moscow a few years ago. I was commenting to a physician who was giving me a guided tour of a medical facility, that it was good sign to see they had FAX machines to improve communications. He leaned close to me and whispered into my ear, "Yes, but we can only receive, they do not yet let us send messages."

Third World countries, regardless of how primitive, usually have many churches. Most churches are well net-worked.

Make contact with a church of any denomination and you will likely get all the help you need. Again, these situations are extremely rare, and if the organization sponsoring you is in the least credible, you should know what to expect long before you leave home.

If all else fails, remember - *"This too shall pass!"* As long as you can say that to yourself you will survive. Actual survival will doubtfully be the problem. The worst scenario will possibly be that you can't complete your original mission. Just do the best you can, make the best of the adventure, think of all the great stories you'll be able to tell your friends, and continue to realize ... *"This too shall pass!"*

Be Prepared:
Volunteers To The World "Take List...."

The following list is compiled from inventories made up by several experienced volunteers to all parts of the primitive world. It is doubtful you would want to take all the listed items, and probably you'll think of several things that are unlisted that are of importance to you. This is intended as a check list to make your adventure more interesting and easy.

1. Toilet Paper.

Do not expect to find toilet paper waiting for you in the Third World. If it is there it will not be of the quality you are used to. Take at least a role per person for each week you'll be in the area. It's no fun to be in the bush without it!

2. Flashlight.

A small flashlight with a good beam is a must. There are several very small pen light size flashlights with focusable beams on the market now, readily available in sporting goods stores. Take along extra batteries and bulbs. Remember, in hot, humid climates, batteries do not last as long and replacements may be unavailable there.

3. Matches or butane lighters.

If you take matches dip the tips in melted wax to waterproof them. High humidity or rain forest weather can render matches useless otherwise.

4. Personal medications.

If you are on medications, naturally you will take them along, but also take along some emergency meds for yourself and your party. <u>Do not - I repeat - do not</u> give these to anyone else under any circumstances. They are for you in an emergency. If you give them up to someone else and then are taken ill and can't work, you will have wasted a good part of your mission. Consider taking such meds as anti-diarrhea medications, broad spectrum antibiotics, digestive aids, antihistamines, analgesics, sleeping aids, antiseptics, laxatives (yes, constipation occurs almost as often as the other), anti-nauseants and motion sickness meds, etc.

5. Cameras, film and TV tape.

No matter where you'll be assigned, the best of

places or the worst of places, you'll see some new and spectacular things. You'll want to record them for yourself and those who'll want to experience your trip vicariously when you come back. If your cameras are not digital be sure to take more film and tape than you think you'll need. You can always bring film and tape back home, but there's nothing more frustrating than running short in the midst of a true adventure. Even if you can find a place to buy your film and tape there, it may be twice or three times the price as in the USA. It may also be long outdated. Cameras and film are not big sellers in the Third World.

If you have motion picture or video equipment with good batteries, take them. You may or may not have outlets to recharge your batteries. Try to find out before you go. I'd also suggest a few rolls of slide film and some ASA 1000 film. Don't let the ASA 1000 go through the luggage X-ray at airports. Of course digital eliminates the film problems, but take extra batteries and storage media, such as disks or SD cards. When you get back, people will ask you to give lectures and slide shows. There will be some poorly lit places which will not lend themselves to flash. If you go in a party, each person should carry cameras and you should have each take a different kind of picture so you can exchange and combine afterwards. That way everyone gets into the pictures. Too often, you the photographer never gets in a photo.

6. Batteries.
If you take anything requiring batteries make sure

you take extras along. Remember, batteries do not last as long in hot, humid climates. If you can find your size batteries in the places you may be going, they will probably not be fresh, they will be very expensive and not the quality you can take from home. Store them in the coolest, driest place you can find.

7. Current converter.

Most places you go to will have some form of electric current. It may be from a makeshift gas powered generator, but it will be electricity. Your problem may be converting it to useable power for your equipment. There are numerous types of small converter kits available on the market. As an afterthought, for women volunteers or women accompanying volunteers, hair curlers often cause problems with foreign current and of course won't work at all when there is no current. Let me suggest a butane curling iron. They are great for travel, even in the USA.

8. Insect repellent.

Try to find out if you are going to an insect infested area. If yes, take repellent. If in doubt, go ahead and take repellent anyway. A good rule of the thumb is, "the nearer sea level you are, the more insects you'll encounter." I was in Ecuador, right on the equator, as tropical latitude as you can get; yet we encountered no insects. We were in a little village in the Andean Mountains at 10,000 feet. Bugs don't like cool thin air. On the other hand I was once assigned to an American

Indian reservation in the north of Montana and was devoured by critters.

There are many brands of insect repellents. The best I've found is not an insect repellent at all. Avon makes a skin product called <u>Skin So Soft</u>; it is by far the best and least expensive insect repellent I've ever tried. Anyone I've ever talked to who tried <u>Skin So Soft</u> to repel insects has testified the same. Also, a word to the wise, in insect country do not wear perfumes or after shave, or use fragrant soaps. The bugs will think you're a flower and come to drink your nectar.

9. Soap.

Take along your favorite unscented soap. The quality of soaps in developing countries and primitive places on this earth is not always to the liking of U.S. Americans. Also, many hotels, bed and breakfast places, hostels and rooming houses, even in "civilized" Europe, do not furnish soap to their boarders. Providing soap is an American custom found mainly in the larger foreign hotels, and even there, quality is not always to our liking. Besides, you'll be staying in very few of those quality hotels.

10. Small towel.

Just as you may not find soap everywhere you go, towels of decent quality may also be scarce. Take one, not your best, along with you. I stayed in the biggest hotel in Moscow, right at Red Square and just before the Iron Curtain came down. I was unpleasantly surprised to find their towels were made of old cut up bed sheets the size of our typical dish towel. Not great after a bath or shower. Hopefully they are better today, but I wouldn't bet on it.

11. Vitamins and salt tablets.

Your diet will probably be that of the people in the area you are visiting. Though many areas of the Third World eat more nutritionally correct than we do, the foods often are not varied or to everyone's pallet. A good vitamin/mineral supplement won't hurt. Also, you may be perspiring more than you expect. Some salt tablets in tropical and subtropical areas can be helpful, but don't over do them.

12. Note pad and pencils.

There will constantly be new experiences that you'll want to take notes about. When you go to primitive areas everything is new and different. There will be too much to remember, so take notes! Pencils are better than pens. If you perspire, get caught in a downpour, fall in a stream, lake, or ocean, or get drenched some other way, penciled notes won't run. Ink may become illegibly blurred.

13. Books.

You will probably find yourself with periods of time, some short and some long, between work periods, at the end of days or while traveling. Boredom can be devastating. Take books. If you're not a reader, become one. At night you'll probably need a reading light. A small high intensity lamp is ideal. You can find some that fold up very small for packing. There are reading lights that operate on batteries and attach right to the cover of the book. I've never found one that worked well enough. Test it out before you go if you plan to take one with you. After you're there is no time to discover I'm right.

Remember extra batteries and bulbs!

14. Language dictionary.
No comment necessary.

15. Language tapes or CD's.
What a great time to learn a new language.

16. Tools of your trade.
Unless you've been assured that adequate diagnostic and minor surgical equipment, or whatever the tools of your trade are will be available, take along a minimum of your own. Nothing is more useless than a physician, dentist, nurse or tradesman without minimal tools. If you have old but useful equipment, take that along. You may even consider leaving it behind for the next volunteer or even a local you've trained in its use; and be able to take a tax deduction for the contribution. Make contributions through the organization that sent you so the deduction will be legal. Also check with your airline, they may forgo the excess luggage fee if they know you are taking supplies for a volunteer mission. They've done it for me on several occasions. You may need a letter from your sponsoring organization to satisfy them that you're not trying to pull a fast one.

17. Personal cassette player and tapes, CD player or Ipod.

It drives me crazy to see people walking around our cities mesmerized by the music coming through their earphones as they stroll down a busy street or through a park, but in the Third World these type items and radio might be ideal. With some of your favorite music, language, books on tape or CD ... it may bring civilization, <u>as you know and perceive it</u>, to the most primitive places. Remember extra batteries.

18. Radio with short wave band.

If you can take a small radio with short wave band you may be able to pick up Voice of America or other distant stations. You may end up hundreds of miles from a broadcast source, but you'll be amazed at how far you can pick up stations, especially at night, with a small short wave band radio.

19. Self sealing plastic baggies.

These are remarkably water, moisture, bug and dirt proof. If you go into rainy or humid areas you will find a hundred uses for them. They will keep equipment, as well as food, clean and dry. They will also keep bugs out of opened food packages. They take up little space and weigh almost nothing. Take several sizes.

20. Typewriter or word processor or <u>whatever</u>.

Don't laugh. I used to carry a typewriter everywhere, which I've now replaced with a lap top word processor. But then I'm a writer, and writers are somewhat nuts. The point is, <u>whatever</u> your passions and pursuits are, there may be a way to take them with you. My lap top word processor lets me pursue my work anyplace in the world. I can even write on flights. If you have a pursuit as important to you as writing is to me, try to figure a way to take it with you. Today's electronic wizardry may provide a way. If you're an artist, take your supplies. I know a physician who is a fine wood carver. He takes his minimal tools to whittle away the long hours of spare time and leaves his products with the local friends he's made. They'll never forget him.

21. Swimsuits.

Even if you don't plan to take a dip, a couple of swim suits may come in very handy. You may find your favorite bath tub is a pond or spring. A swimsuit may be the handiest sleeping apparel. Always carry one in your day pack and carry-on luggage.

22. Snorkel and dive equipment

If you are traveling near bodies of water and are a snorkeler of diver, don't miss the opportunities. Take your equipment.

23. Sunglasses and extra prescription glasses

If you are dependent on eye wear, never leave home without a spare pair as well as a copy of your prescription. Sunglasses are a necessity in most places. You'll probably be spending a great deal of your time outside. That may be where you practice your trade.

24. Binoculars

If you have them take them ... if you don't have a pair, buy or borrow. There's bound to be something you'd like to see up closer.

25. Playing cards and games

Even solitaire can be a mind saver at times. If you play chess take a small set.

26. Utility pocket knife

A Swiss Army knife or comparable device can come in very handy in primitive areas.

27. Nail clippers and file

Nothing seems worse than a broken nail or hangnail that you can't take care of.

28. Sewing kit and extra buttons

Should need no explanation.

29. Small mirror

Ever try to shave, comb your hair or put on makeup without one? Metal is better than glass.

30. Rain wear

A plastic poncho type rain cape that folds into a small packet and can be carried in your pocket may save you hours of discomfort in the field some day.

31. Day pack

Put a small back pack or fanny pack that will fold up in your luggage, to be brought out when you need to carry just enough junk to get through the day in the field. This day pack is also good for a day of sightseeing or shopping in the big city or market town.

32. Very comfortable walking shoes

This is a must in the city or in the field. You will be on your feet more than you can imagine.

You may have to walk many miles every day on every kind of terrain. **Get a shoe that is light in weight that breathes, gives good arch support, and has a very soft cushion heel, and sturdy but flexible non-skid traction sole.**

Above all, make sure the fit is comfortable. A very good (not necessarily the most expensive) running or competitive walking shoe is best in almost all terrain where you aren't into deep mud or snow. For mud and snow waterproof boots will probably be best.

33. Family photos

Pictures of your family and loved ones can be a tremendous morale booster, and the people you will be working with will want to see your family pictures if your family is not accompanying you.

34. Basic first aid kit

Even if you may have a clinic or hospital full of

equipment available to you if you're a doctor, nurse or dentist, a basic first aid kit that you can throw into your day pack at the last minute, might be very helpful.

35. Travel alarm and waterproof watch

I recommend an inexpensive dive watch with a dual time movement so that you can tell at a glance what time it is back home without a lot of calculation, should you want to call home at a convenient time.

36. A telephone credit card

It will amaze you that telephone credit card numbers work in a majority of developing countries. Never, never, never make a long distance call from a foreign country that isn't a credit card or collect call. Telephone long distance rates in foreign countries usually are many, many times more expensive than U.S. rates. I know one volunteer who made a call home from Athens, Greece and was shocked by a charge of $127.00, ten times what the same call would have cost if billed at home.

37. If you play a musical instrument try to take it along.

Music is a universal language and can make for fun and friends in a hurry. Hope your instrument isn't a piano or organ.

Take blank checks.

With your blank check and a major credit card you can buy extra emergency money in most major banks or credit card offices in foreign countries.

G.P.S. or Global Positioning System.

If you have one take it. It's always nice to know where you are, and more than one life's been saved with these gadgets. You might want a compass too.

These are things that volunteers I've crossed paths with over the years found helpful in making their missions more productive and pleasant. If you took everything on this list you'd have to have an elephant for a pack animal. Actually, you will most likely be the pack animal. You wouldn't take everything in this list on every mission, and you'll surely have things you want to add to the list. Look upon this as a check list you will pick from and add to. When you are out on your missions add things to the inventory list you wish you had with you to jog your memory for the next time. Learn from your trial and error. Better yet learn from the trial and error of others.

Luggage

Let's take a few moments to talk about luggage.

Avoid fancy luggage. Take practical. Old stuff is perhaps best. It may be bounced around in trucks, on top of busses, in all kinds of weather, carried by natives, strapped on the sides of donkeys, thrown into open boats, stashed in small or vintage aircraft. In other words, don't take your best new luggage.

Also take as few pieces as you can get by with. Remember, you may be carrying it yourself from time to time. Essentials and valuables should best be kept in your carry on luggage at all times. Cameras, radios, Ipod, computers, electronic equipment and the like are a tremendous temptation to airport baggage handlers anywhere, not only in primitive areas.

It is also wise to carry an extra change of clothes with you. All too often, one or more pieces of your luggage will get delayed and you may find yourself with just the clothes on your back for several days. Take a change you can wear while the wash dries.

Carry an extra duffel bag. Invariably, when in a strange country, especially as different as most Third World countries are, you will find many souvenirs to bring back with you. Some may just be oddities unique to a strange place, others may be fantastic bargains. While in Ecuador I discovered that hand made wool sweaters, ponchos, and shawls were not only beautifully colorful, but a fraction of the cost of woolens in the US. The bargains were too tempting. Even taking extra gear with me to take home such items, I had to buy baggage to carry back the "loot." Luckily, leather goods in Ecuador were also a bargain and I got a fantastic buy on terrific luggage. Light weight nylon or nylon-like baggage that folds flat and fits easily into your other luggage is the ideal type of extra duffel. It is also convenient for storage of your dirty laundry while on assignments.

Above all try to go as light as you can. My wife and I traveled three weeks in Botswana, South Africa and were limited to just 26 pounds of luggage each because of the small aircraft we had to fly in. It was the lightest my wife had ever traveled, but we made it just fine.

CHAPTER 4

GETTING THERE

The quickest way between two points is a straight line. But when you're trying to get somewhere in the Third World it never seems to work that way. Connections never appear to be simple. You usually have to overnight in one or more primitive locales and it's rare that you can make it on two air carriers, much less one. Chances are a good portion of the trip will be on an airline or charter even your travel agent hasn't ever heard of. But look upon that as part of the adventure.

In addition to "Puddle Jumper Airline" you may travel in native dug-out canoe, primitive bus, truck, Jeep, antique car, open boat, wagon, horse or donkey, mule back, mountain railroad, on foot, or by any other imaginable conveyance. It's all part of the exploit. In transit you may mutter, many times, "This too shall pass!" And it will. And after it's over you'll remember it fondly as an important part of the whole experience.

While in transit you'll likely spend nights and often some days waiting in some spot on this earth you'd never ever expect to be. Carry books, camera, or whatever your favorite time passer might be. Times in these places need never be wasted. Be willing to explore. Look upon these <u>stranded</u> moments as opportunities. Try to understand the lives of the people native to the area. Inquire. Mingle. Make friends. If the occasion is there, travel out into the region around the spot in which you've had to "lay over."

If you have a favorite travel agent, let him or her have some of the pleasure of planning your transportation. A phone call will get the ball rolling. They will probably have no problem getting you on the proper continent, but then the going may get a little tough. Foreign airlines fly some strange schedules. You may be lucky to get out of the U.S. on the same day you leave home. I wish I had a dollar for every time I've had to lay over in Miami on my way to South America, Central America or the Caribbean. I suggest that you have your travel agent contact the organization sending you. Unless you are the first to go to your destination, that organization probably knows the intricacies of getting there and will share it with your agent, saving their trial and your error. If you're lucky your sponsor organization will make the best travel arrangements for you.

Once you arrive in your foreign port of entry, your commute adventure really starts.

Major cities will probably have some nice hotels. They may be more expensive than you expect. If an organization is paying your way your stay will probably be in a cheaper room. You may or may not have a private bathroom. The sheets should be clean but may be a bit thread bear. If they are clean, don't complain. Remember, this may be your best accommodation for a while. Savor it! It is likely you'll be looking forward to getting back to a room like this in the near future.

It is impossible to predict now what your next form of travel will be. If your travel agent was able to make the arrangements, you won't be surprised, but often your arrangements from this point on will be taken care of by your hosts. They may not even be sure yet how to get you to the point where you'll deliver your services. "Roll with the punches." Be gracious. You may get picked up in a thirty year old truck. If it runs, count your blessings. If it doesn't, read your book, or better yet, see if you can help solve the problem. Be flexible. Seek out the humor. It's there. A sense of humor is your best ticket to a good time in developing countries. Above all, learn not to look at your watch too often. Learn to ignore time. Third World time is a very nebulous, vague, foggy, indefinite, low priority thing. If you are a slave to time you'll go nuts in the Third World.

Don't be surprised if you have to do some walking. In Honduras I once had to walk an average of twelve miles a day from jungle village to jungle village to deliver medical care. I've known volunteers who trekked three days in the Himalayas of Nepal to get to the clinic where they could do their work. All along the way people stopped them to get roadside medical care and advice. It was a satisfying experience for the volunteers and a real service to the mountain villagers. And just think of the memories.

It's important you have good walking shoes, well broken in before you leave home. The bush is no place to develop a blister. Chances are you won't have to trek through a jungle or up a mountain, but wherever you do go you can bet you'll walk more than you do at home. You'll want to! You'll love it, and walking is the best exercise you can do. <u>Again, make sure you have a good pair of walking shoes!</u>

In Honduras I was also asked to travel by open boat along the Atlantic coast and up rivers in dugout canoes, so don't be surprised at anything they put you in. Your sponsoring organization should be able to forewarn or prepare you unless you're the first to go into a new area. Whatever way you are asked to travel, it's probably the best they have in these areas. Be a sport about it. Be gracious! Again, if this kind of roughing it isn't for you, no need to apologize or worry about it, just seek out a volunteer mission less threatening. I'll bet you can find one in your own city which may only require you to take a bus from near your house if you don't want to drive yourself.

But, thank the Lord, in most places you'll do better. Inland bus or train transportation is very common, although they are not necessarily busses and trains as we know them here. Third World busses are more like our school busses - very old school busses! Some busses are open, without windows or doors, or even sides in some cases. At least they do usually have a top!

Some busses are kind of like flat bed trucks with benches. But they get you there. And don't be too surprised if the guy next to you has a pig, big fish or sack of live chickens on his lap.

Speaking of big fish and chickens, you'll get your indoctrination to your new diet on your trip to your assignment. Third World food is not usually five star continental dining, but it is usually nutritionally good; better nutritionally than most American diets provide, especially if you frequent fast food places. Often it is healthier than our typical American household diet. Third World diets are usually boring compared to ours. There isn't much variety unless you are on an island or coast where many species of fish and sea foods are available. In Honduras I ate beans and rice three times a day for three weeks. That was extreme, and thank the Lord for other dietary experiences!

Actually, Third World Food is usually high in fiber, and low in cholesterol and fat. You'll find little beef or red meat, lots of chicken and fish when meat is available, and sometimes pork or lamb and goat. Rice and beans are usually part of every meal. Fruits and vegetables vary with the regions. You'll experience fruits we haven't even heard of here in the U.S. All in all, Third World food will be an interesting experience to you.

When you finally get to your destination, your home away from home may also be a surprise.

Be prepared for primitive living conditions and you won't end up shocked or too disappointed. In my experiences I've slept in some unbelievable places, such as in a jungle hammock under a tree in a Honduras Contra encampment, on the floor of a warehouse with a sack of rice as my pillow, on a cowhide stretched as tight as a drum on a wood frame in a native thatch hut on stilts, and in a dormitory style lodging of a United Nations refugee camp. I've also been housed in a three bedroom apartment, a four bedroom house with two bathes, a three bedroom house with three baths, a very comfortable trailer home, in a quaint cabin of hewn logs, in hospital intern quarters, in rooms of local hotels and several times in homes of the natives of the countries I've served.

There were a very few places I've stayed to which I'd just as soon not return, but honestly, I can't think of one place I'm sorry I had to endure at the time I was there. As bad and primitive as some of the places sound, I've always been made as comfortable as anyone else in the society or community I've visited. When in Rome you'll live as a Roman, when in the jungle you'll experience jungle life. It's all part of the adventure and usually the best part of it. You'll be amazed at your own adaptability. You'll learn things about yourself you never knew, and you'll be proud you did!

You'll hopefully let yourself be a part of the community you are visiting. If you're not, it will probably be your own fault. The people will likely invite you in with open arms. Jump right in. But stay out of the politics. It's alright to listen and be an uninvolved observer, but do not voice your own opinions if you can avoid it. Your job is to function as an unbiased provider of services to the people and if you get involved in issues of political nature you will probably diminish your effectiveness and perhaps invite trouble.

Politics in foreign countries are not like politics here in the United States. In some places they play politics with their lives. Also, you can't enter into a discussion of foreign politics with American values. They don't necessarily fit in everywhere, even though you'd like to think they do. You may think you have a solution to all their problems, but you'll be wise to keep those solutions to yourself. Your hosts may want to know all about life and politics in the U.S. and its usually good to share this with them; just don't get involved with how you think they should run their country. To do your best work you should be as apolitical as possible. The same goes for religious matters. You can share your views and beliefs with them if they ask, but don't critique their beliefs or try to proselytize. To think your religious views are better than theirs is in my view to be looked upon as arrogance.

Get to know the people and let them know you. Be honest with them. Don't talk down to them or be superior. Answer their questions but don't boast about your "good life" in the states. Constant comparison of life back home to their lifestyle will not endear you to them. Point out the similarities and emphasize values you share with them.

See as much as you can of the country. Ask them to show you as much as they can. Let them know you are sincerely interested in them, their lives, their homes and their country. Make them feel you are there because you want to be there, not just to help them and teach them. Let them know you want to learn from them and take good memories back home with you. With the proper attitude you will learn far more than you teach, you will take back with you far more than you leave with them.

Again, "When in Rome..." is still pretty good advice!

CHAPTER 5

GOING IN A GROUP, TAKING FAMILY

If you can take your spouse, the family, friends or go in a group, that's wonderful, usually. However, a few words of warning. Make sure you go to a post where everyone will be happy. You may be all charged up to the adventure to come, but is everyone else interested in your kind of exploit? Don't forget, you will be busy a good part of the time with your service work. That could spell hours of boredom for spouse and family. Make sure they are aware of what your schedule might be so they can prepare for activities during those periods. If possible get them involved in the work as well.

Frequently the group sending you might have some worthwhile work for them, too. Why should you be the only one to get satisfaction from helping others? My organization, Doctors To The World, purposely started two other organizations, Volunteers To The World and Student Volunteers To The World, just so that non-medical persons accompanying our medical personnel could also get involved. Since then, both Volunteers To The World and Student Volunteers To The World have developed a substantial membership of their own and offer projects unrelated to our medical programs.

It is just as important that those accompanying you know as much as they can about where they are going and what they should expect. If their hearts aren't in your plans, then reconsider taking them, or better yet select a different assignment where all of you will have a chance at being happy.

If there are doubts and mixed feelings about accompanying you on a long assignment, they may want to keep open the option of returning earlier than you, should things not work out. Perhaps they could take time out to travel to other interesting spots in the vicinity while you continue doing your thing. The option of lengthening their and your stay may also be desirable.

There are few bad assignments, but sometimes there are mismatched assignments. No matter how wonderful you think an assignment is, there are those who would have hated every minute of it.

An assignment you consider the pits is sure to be someone else's perfect situation. Make sure that if several of you are going, everyone is reasonably well matched to the situations you'll be facing. The advantages of going in a well chosen group are many and obvious. It does take planning, extra preparation and cooperation. Everyone who accompanies you should read through this handbook so they can properly prepare themselves.

One more word of warning when going in a group. Too often when a family or group all go, you will tend to stay with one another too exclusively. *DO NOT LET YOUR GROUP KEEP YOU FROM GETTING OUT AMONG THE PEOPLE!* Getting out among your hosts should be done as a group, and individually! Too often, U.S diplomats in foreign countries stay to themselves in their diplomatic community and compounds. That makes for poor international relations. Never forget that you and your group are very important representatives of the United States, or what ever country you are from, and of the organization sending you in to help. Don't be exclusive and unsocial to your host community. Like them and they will like you, love them and they will love you and all U.S. Americans, or whatever your country might be.

CHAPTER 6

MORE ABOUT AVOIDING CULTURE SHOCK

Culture shock is such a serious matter that it deserves its own chapter. It is a psychological incapacitation brought about by confronting a situation far different from what you really anticipated. Thus, its effects can greatly be diminished or avoided if one does his or her homework to learn as much about the destination or host country as possible. As a hedge against culture shock, it is best to expect the worst. I've never encountered serious or debilitating culture shock in a person who was pleasantly surprised to find a more hospitable destination than was expected.

This is not to say that every place you'll visit in developing countries is a horror show waiting to be discovered. **Quite the contrary, most places will offer delights and experiences beyond your happiest anticipations.**

What I'm saying is that culture shock is brought on more by a state of mind than by actual conditions. I've had minor culture shock on vacations in the U.S.A. when I was expecting a four star hotel and got three star. On the other hand I've been in many a two star hotel without turning a hair when all I expected was one or two star. I'll bet you have had the same experience. Get a four star facility when you're expecting a five star vacation, especially at a five star price, and from then on everything seems to go down hill.

Even though culture shock is a mental and emotional condition, it can be devastating and it can make you totally ineffective in the work you expected to do. It can prevent you from having any pleasure from your volunteer experiences. If you can't perform your intended tasks or enjoy yourself, the trip will be a waste of your time, talent and someone's money. On the other hand if you know what to expect, and go prepared to be challenged by the very worst, you'll probably be pleasantly surprised, do a terrific job, have a wonderful time and have great stories to tell for a lifetime.

In other words, the best defense against culture shock is not in overcoming the situations once you've encountered them, but in careful preparation of your expectations and equipment before you leave home. Correctly anticipating problems means going prepared to cope and avert culture shock. Improper anticipation and preparation means having to cope with problems of all degrees of seriousness under less than favorable conditions, and perhaps being ill equipped to handle them. That adds up to severe culture shock.

So how does one prepare for venturing into underdeveloped areas? We've touched a little on it already in Chapter 3, Preparation. We'll review the high points and touch on some other hints and details in this section.

Since most developing countries have little tourism, you'll probably find little written about them in the usual sources. I don't believe Arthur Frommer has written on "How To See Zona Miskito On $5 and $10 Dollars a Day!" He hasn't because there are too few places in Zona Miskito of Honduras or Nicaragua where you can find an establishment to take your five or ten tourist dollars. And I'll bet there isn't one travel agency in twenty that has ever heard of Zona Miskito, much less that can give you any information about the area or book you into it. But there are still ways to research and prepare for Zona Miskito or the many wonderful primitive and less explored places on this planet.

National Geographic Magazine, as I've mentioned before, is a wonderful source of information on some of the more remote places on earth. This magnificent publication has been printed since 1888 and is completely indexed from volume I, Issue I. Look up your destination in the collection in your public library. You may find an article written as long as fifty years ago, but read it. As I said before, things change very slowly in the Third World. In most developing countries little has changed in centuries, much less in fifty years. And if there have been dramatic changes they should be for the better. That will make your anticipated no star experience a delightful one or two star adventure. Better to be over prepared then under equipped.

Another great resource is the Internet. In fact, the Internet may be the best source of material on remote places. Try searching on the name of the location where you will be stationed, the name of the group of people there, or on any related subject you can think of. As you discover information about your destination, one search result can easily lead to another, and soon you will start to piece together some useful knowledge of the place. Google search, and Google Images are two great places to begin your Internet research. Be aware that National Geographic itself provides some good content on their website too.

The best information about the area may be available from the organization sending you in. Any organization worth its salt should investigate any area to which they send personnel with an on-site inspection and evaluation. If they don't know what they are sending you into, reconsider. In addition, most good volunteer organizations get reports from volunteers who have gone in before. These valuable comments should be made available to all potential volunteers to follow. They should give you a very clear picture of what to expect - what problems you'll encounter, what equipment and supplies you need take, etc. The organization should have no qualms about giving you the names, addresses and phone numbers of volunteers who have been there. Call them and ask, ask, ask! Let your spouse ask too! No question that enters your mind should go unasked. If you can't think of questions on your own here are a few things you should wonder about:

1. Just how primitive is the area?
2. What's the weather like?
3. What are the people like?
4. What will they expect of me?
5. What are the major problems I'll be confronting?
6. What clothing should I take?
7. What equipment should I take?
8. What surprises should I expect?
9. How much money should I take?
10. What currency do they use and where is the best place to get it?
11. What health problems might I encounter and what personal medications should I take?
12. What will my living conditions be like?
13. What can you tell me about the food and water?
14. What type insect and animal life should I expect?
15. What facilities are there to buy everyday needs such as film, batteries, toilet paper, soap, foods, etc?
16. Will I have to take my own linens and towels?
17. What kind of transportation is available there and how much will I be traveling once there?

18. What do you recommend for leisure time activities?

19. Tell me a little about the politics?

20. What are the major religions there?

21. Are there any local mores I need to watch out for?

22. Are the people friendly?

23. Is there anything you would have done differently?

24. Would you go back for another tour? If not, why?

25. Is there a language problem?

26. Is crime a problem and what precautions are wise or necessary?

These are a few of the questions you might consider asking. Let the flow of conversation dictate any other questions that may come up. Again, the organization sending you should be able to answer all the above from their own first hand on site investigation of the area. But even if they do, get another opinion from a volunteer. From two or more volunteers is even better, especially if the first report is extreme, whether for or against. Remember that individual differences have as much to do with recommendations as the experiences people have. Gather as many facts as you can from as many sources as you can, then draw your own conclusions.

If, after you've investigated and interrogated, you feel the place is not for you or for your family or other companions, I suggest you reconsider. There are thousands of places in this world that can use your help. Pick one you'll be compatible with and like. Leave the others to those compatible with them. You owe it to yourself and the people you'll be serving and having to deal with. You'll do the best job where you can be happy. Select carefully, especially if it's your first experience in developing countries. Make it easy on yourself. A few suggestions:

1. Pick a place where there is no language problem for you, where English is spoken or you are proficient in the host country's foreign language.

2. Try to find a climate where you'll be comfortable. If you prefer cool dry weather don't pick a hot steamy jungle the first time out. It will just compound your other problems.

3. If you're a fastidious person, don't select an assignment where you'll be living in squalor and poverty. But keep in mind that poverty and primitive are not at all synonymous. There are very primitive places where the people are neat, clean, hygienic and as fastidious as you are. In fact, slums are seldom found in developing countries; they are more often a product of class distinctions in more modern nations.

4. For your first few trips try to go with a group of volunteers who have an experienced leader, to an assignment that has a fairly structured program.

5. Try to get stationed near a large community

where you'll have more support systems available to you.

6. Don't obligate yourself to too long a mission the first time. You can stand almost anything if it's for just a few weeks. It should be short enough to make your "This too shall pass" not too long and keep it believable.

7. Look for an assignment offering activities and interests to occupy your free time. *On your first assignment think of yourself first.* True altruism can come after you've broken yourself in.

8. Select a location which enables you to communicate with home and the outside world. When I was in Zona Miskito, Honduras I was unable to contact the outside world for three weeks until I finally ran across a radio operator who got a message to my home via Ham Radio operators in the U.S. Of all the hardships of that primitive area, the inability to let my family know where I was and that I was safe and in good health, concerned me most.

9. To some people, insects and other small creatures seem to be a horrendous threat. Developing countries seem to have more than their fair share of creepers and crawlies. The great majority of these critters take absolutely no interest in us humans. Get yourself a book on insects, another on small reptiles and one that covers small mammals, especially rodents. First, you'll

discover that almost none can or want to do you in. That will be a tremendous relief to you. Secondly, once you start to know something about the "itsy bitsy" animal kingdom, your revulsion of it will turn to fascination. *Any kid who ever had an ant farm isn't bothered by ants!*

10. Try to develop an interest in nature, such as plants, shells, sea life, birds, astronomy, etc. A person with broad interests is more likely to feel at home no matter where in the world he or she finds him or herself. If the kids are to accompany you, get them interested too. This can be one of the greatest learning experiences they will ever have.

11. For your own self confidence, read through a survival manual. You'll probably never get lost or be totally reliant on your own skills for survival, but it can't hurt to know how to make it on your own and you'll feel better for it. A Boy Scout manual has lots of good survival information easily explained. Military survival manuals are also readily available.

12. Once again, learn as much about the places you'll be going, before you leave. For your first mission, you may want to pick an assignment right here in the U.S.A or what ever your home country might be. There is plenty of need to be filled right at home!

Culture shock can be prevented or kept to a minimum, but if you travel enough, be it volunteering, on the job, or as a tourist, it will eventually get you. When it does, here are the few steps that will help you overcome it:

1. Stop everything and think about what factors are causing your problems.

2. Don't try to solve everything at once! Prioritize your list of obstacles and try to resolve the worst first.

3. Inventory your assets. Don't focus just on your problems. That's depressing and tends to handicap you further. Start to make a list, mentally or on paper, of all the resources at your disposal and get on top of the situation.

4. If you can't solve the worst challenge first, don't dwell on it, try to resolve the next, and so on down the list. Culture shock is the worst when you let several problems overwhelm you. Get focused on one problem at a time and you can lick almost anything.

5. Try to find humor in your situation. Think of the great stories you'll be able to tell when you get back home. "Make lemonade of your lemons!" Most situations aren't nearly as bad as we first think they are. Very often it is our own egos that cause us the biggest problems. We feel we deserve better, so we expect better and thus we find it difficult to cope with second best - which is usually still pretty good.

6. Often, culture shock happens when you are fatigued, especially after exhaustion from long and difficult travel. If you are especially tired, get rest before you tackle your culture shock problems. Almost every situation looks better in the morning.

No matter how well we prepare before we leave home for a destination, we are all subject to occasional culture shock, no matter how experienced we may be in world travel. Don't think less of yourself when it happens to you. The trick is to recognize it and cope with it when it hits. Always remember, "It too will pass!"

CHAPTER 7

MEET THE COMPETITION, GREET THE MEDICINE CHIEF

As much as the people you're going to help might appreciate and love you for what you are doing, there's someone out there who may view you as a threat. He or she or they may well be your competition. In my case it's usually the local medical community.

On a few occasions I've gone into areas where there was no medical care, at least as we know medical care. Even in the most medically deprived areas, someone has always been designated or looked upon as "health practitioner." It may have been an old matriarch who over the years has been asked advice from others because she seemed to have healing powers, or had learned about the plants and herbs from her mother or grandmother. Or it may have been someone formally designated as "The Medicine Chief." Regardless of what their title is, or how they got it, or how they practice their craft, <u>make them your ally</u>! I may have been the hottest doc in the area once I arrived, but without the friendship and support and good wishes of the "Medicine Chief" I wouldn't stand a chance in hell of accomplishing my goals.

If the best that people have had in the past was someone sprinkling "magic potions" on their ailing bodies while a mystic dance or chant was taking place, then they probably have lots of faith in that "mystic." After all, 90% of our patients get well in spite of us doctors, not because of us. The mystics probably have at least as good a track record, and they dance a lot better than we do. If I want to do a better job on the remaining 10% of the patients who actually get better <u>because</u> of us, then I'd better get the cooperation of the competition first.

Whatever your skill or service, someone else has probably been doing it all along, if on a more primitive basis. If that person feels threatened by you because you may put him or her out of business or show them to be less of a practitioner than yourself, you'll have an enemy ready to scuttle your boat at every turn. After all, you're not going to your assignment to put anyone else out of business.

Just like us doctors here in the modern world, all the Medicine Chiefs I've run into had a huge ego. Meet them on their own turf, don't talk down to them, let them know that *you want to help them do their job* as best you can; that you want to *work with them* as a team and that you want to *learn from them* whatever you can and are willing to teach them anything you can of your own skills.

If you don't convince them that you aren't there to put them down or out, you're going to have problems. That's among the primitives. In less primitive areas the situation is actually far worse. When I go into an area where there are "real" doctors, their perceived threat is much greater. I have to prove that I'm not there to take the bread from their table and to steal their thunder. I must convince them that what I hope to do will not disrupt the economy of the existing medical community but is only intended to ease their work burden.

In addition, I must make them understand that they will not be diminished in the esteem of their patients. These are reasonable concerns. If I don't convince them, their "board of health" will probably bar me from practicing my skills in their community. Our state medical boards do the same to protect us from "invasion of foreign doctors." We aren't that different from the "Medicine Chief!"

Keep in mind, that when I or all the other volunteer physicians leave the area, all that the locals will have will be their Medicine Chiefs. If we've shaken their faith in the only medical provider there, we've done everyone a great disservice. On the other hand, if we've worked with the Medicine Chief, within his or her system, and in such a way that we've increased his or her knowledge and skills and prestige, then we've accomplished our mission.

If you're a carpenter, you may pose the same threat to anyone who has been building homes and furniture in the area in the past. Allying your self with that party or parties can only benefit you. It all starts with a common courtesy call.

CHAPTER 8

TSUTSUGAMUSHI WHAT?

We've said a lot about learning as much as you can about the region, its people, their politics, the climate, and so on. Just as important, you should try to find out about the practice of your skills in the host area where you will be plying your trade. Too often we are so enamored by our own brilliance that we assume we're prepared to do our jobs flawlessly when we get there. Do yourself a favor and <u>prepare a little more!</u> Ask at least two questions. One, what endemic problems exist there? Two, how has it been taken care of until now? If Tsutsugamushi Fever is an endemic disease in the area and you can find that out before you go, you'll be able to refresh yourself all about that remote disease and its treatment before you leave home.

If you're a carpenter and you can find out that the major building material in the host area is bamboo and that through the centuries it has been held together by leather thongs or some kind of twine you may have a chance to read up on the properties of bamboo, how to work with it - and save yourself a hell of a shock when you get there and discover there are no boards to nail together.

How do you find out about Tsutsugamushi Fever and bamboo?

The Internet is a great resource of course, but even more importantly, start by asking the organization sending you. Ask those who went ahead of you. Also, read the encyclopedia, *National Geographic Magazine*, check in the public library, call your Public Health Department, World Health Organization of the United Nations, the Anthropology Department of your local college or someone else's local college. It may take a little digging if you can't get the information from your sponsor group or your predecessors. Again, wonder about any sponsoring organization that can't give you the basic facts you need to know about the place they are sending you!

We who live in the modern high-tech world, especially we U.S. Americans, have an inclination to assume that the way we do anything is the best or only way of doing it. Don't be too sure.

What works here doesn't always work as well in the Third World. High-tech fails in the Third World as often, if not more often, than it works.

I can't begin to tell you how much high tech equipment I've seen in developing countries, gathering dust because it couldn't be maintained, couldn't get started, was missing a 29 cent part that couldn't be replaced, had no one trained to operate it, was incompatible with the local power source, wouldn't work in the temperature or humidity, couldn't be shielded from vermin that insisted on living in its inner workings, shorted out everything when ever it was turned on, blows its fuses every time it was turned on, came without instructions, etc., etc,. etc. ad infinitum.

In developing countries and disaster areas, simple is usually best.

If the locals build with bamboo, frapped with vines or leather, and have done so for four centuries, there is probably a good reason for it. Perhaps the wood of the area is too hard to work with. Perhaps nails and screws are too costly, too unavailable, too easily rusted out, too dependent on tools not readily available. Perhaps bamboo is easier to replenish or longer lasting.

Whatever the reason, there is a reason why people traditionally do the things they do. Don't insist on changes unless you are very sure they are for the best. Ask why they don't before you suggest they do - why they do when you think they shouldn't.

Many, if not most American doctors tend to doubt the value of acupuncture, a form of health care that has survived in the orient for thousands of years. Ask those doctors why they think acupuncture is foolish and they won't have a scientific reason.

Usually the visitor's pooh-pooh it because they don't understand it. But something that has survived four thousand years, in spite of not having an easy explanation, deserves more than to be summarily dismissed. I've seen it do wonders. I can't explain it. I'm not ready to embrace it, practice it, or change my own practice methods for it, but I sure am fascinated by it, am more than willing to coexist with it, and would be happy to learn more about it from a master practitioner of acupuncture.

When the locals do something differently from you, learn as much from them about their methods as you can - their whys and hows. You'll be a better person for it in most cases. Once you've learned as much as you can, with an open mind, you'll be that much better able to argue your own points, if you're still so inclined. However, I'll bet that as often as not, you'll discover some good reasons for "their madness."

In Honduras I met a medicine chief who treats malaria with a tea he brews from a local plant. I can't explain how it works, or even verify for sure if it works, but I didn't see any of his people suffering of malaria. I wish I could have had a cup of his tea when I had malaria that I caught while in his area. It took three different tries to get rid of it with our modern drugs.

Keep an open mind and you are bound to learn some interesting things that will be helpful to you even in our modern world. This is not to say you shouldn't teach. Teaching is often the most valuable thing we can do. Just don't take the attitude that our way is the only way, or even the best way. At best it's just another way. Let them have some decision in what's best for them.

CHAPTER 9

DIFFERENT STANDARDS, LEARNING MORE THAN YOU TEACH

When you go to work in developing countries, be flexible. Be prepared to work by different standards. Don't complain if things aren't as perfect as you'd like them to be. The tools of your trade may be more primitive than you would like, the ability of those assisting you may be less exact than you are used to, the facility in which you work may be far more humble than you can imagine, and the expectations of your services may be far short of what you would expect of yourself.

If you do the very best you can with the resources you have you should consider yourself successful. I recall on one occasion in the jungle of Zona Miskito, Honduras, feeling particularly frustrated because I didn't have some simple supplies to treat some minor fungus infections of the skin and a few patients with digestive disorders. As the day drew on, I became more and more depressed at my uselessness. I was able to instruct the natives with the dermatological problems on cleansing the infected areas, drying them well and letting the sun get to the lesions, which would eventually cure the fungus, and I was able to alter the diets of the gastritis patients to ease their symptoms while their illness ran its course, but that wasn't the same as being able to effect the "dramatic cure" we physicians like to take credit for.

The final straw came when a twelve year old girl came into me with a tumor protruding from her left thigh. I envisioned her losing her leg and possibly her life to the growth. She needed a major hospital facility which was not just hundreds of miles away, but days of trekking through jungle and canoeing on rivers to get to a jungle airfield which was the final connection to the outside world.

This Indian village didn't even have radio communication to the outside world. I felt totally helpless and useless. I expressed my feelings of defeat to the young Contra who was my interpreter and guide from village to village. He communicated my statements to his commander and the next thing I knew four Contras came bearing a hammock strung from two long poles they supported from their shoulders. The girl was placed in the hammock and they left carrying her off into the jungle. They carried her fourteen miles through the jungle and then sixteen miles by dugout canoe to a village with an airfield and a radio. A Honduran military aircraft was dispatched for her and in two days she was in a major hospital in

La Ceiba, Honduras. My young interpreter pointed out to me that I was making a difference. "Had you not come here we would not have known to send this young girl to the hospital. And if you brought with you the medicines you needed for the skin and the stomach, we would not have learned how to treat the sickness after you were gone and the medicine was run out!"

We can't always be the heroes we would like to be, so be the next best thing, the hero's fate lets us be.

People in primitive cultures are amazingly resourceful. It is a quality they have developed out of necessity, and that we have practically lost out of overabundance. We U. S. Americans don't too often have to fly by the seat of our pants. We have become so dependent on high tech that we don't often have to think about figuring out solutions. We just order some tests, or put some figures into a calculator, or type a series of variables into a computer, or see how the last guy did it, or look in the books, or pass the problem down to our assistants, or, or, or....

In primitive countries there are seldom tests, calculators, computers, adequate books, previous solutions or knowledgeable assistants available. It is amazing how much I have learned from "primitives" on how to make do, how to improvise, how to prioritize, how to role with the punches, how to survive, how to utilize, how to transpose, how to simplify, how to facilitate, how to expedite, how to substitute, how to subsidize, how to, how to, how to.... I have learned a lot more than I've ever taught! And that's just in regard to my profession! Just as important is what they have taught me in regard to living my life.

Values and priorities have been my greatest compensation for the time I've given to those less fortunate than I. And when I converse with others who have volunteered in developing countries or disasters, every last one has been in full agreement, that nothing has influenced their lives as much as their experiences helping victims of disaster or privation. Nothing will make you appreciate what we have in this country more than working with people who have far less. Nothing will recharge your character more than the realization of how blessed we are in most cases. What we consider creature comfort others look upon as grand luxury.

But everything you will learn will be pleasing, and that is what will reshape your character.

The things we waste every day, others would be elated to have.

You'll come to realize that keeping up with the Joneses is a petty way of setting priorities and values. I'm not saying that luxury isn't pleasant and should never be a goal, but not at the cost of our health, our families or our scruples. Take a hard look around you and see what price some of us pay for the goals we set for ourselves. Then take a critical look at those goals. A few tours of service to others will help you put your values and priorities in their proper places. For our kids whose principles are just taking shape, the Third World experience, either accompanying you or helping in their own right, will be the most valuable parcel of time they will ever have spent.

You'll learn something fascinating in your Third World adventures. Though the people you'll be working with have very little in the way of material wealth, especially compared to what we have here in the U.S.A. or modern world, you will find that often they are far happier than we are in our affluent society. A pleasant evening in most foreign communities is sitting around a table with friends drinking coffee, wine or other refreshment and having a conversation. Most of us can't pull ourselves away from the TV even to talk to our loved ones.

You'll spend more time conversing in a foreign country in one evening than the average U.S. family spends talking to one another in a whole week. It is a sad fact that the average U.S. husband and wife spend less than one hour a week in conversation, and the average father spends less than 30 minutes a week in dialogue with his children. How much time have you spent talking to your family this week? In a foreign place you'll spend hours daily in the good old art of conversation, sometimes with total strangers that have very little in common with you. Here at home we let our luxuries get in the way of the simple things that are <u>really</u> important to us.

When was the last time you just took a walk with your spouse, your kids or a close friend? Golf doesn't count. I mean a walk taken just for the sake of being together to enjoy each other. That's what folks do in foreign countries. I'm not talking just developing countries, I mean in almost all foreign countries, but it is especially true in developing countries. We in the U.S. have lost contact with one another. When it comes to relationships we are a very shallow people. A few tours of duty outside the U.S. will give you and those who accompany you some depth - depth of character and depth as an interested and interesting person.

If the above doesn't seem like much reward to you for the services you will give, then you need the volunteer experience most of all. What you will gain will be something money can never buy. What your kids will learn, no tuition could possibly purchase. What a fantastic payment, just for the Joy of Volunteering!

CHAPTER 10

DISASTERS

Up until now we have been dealing with volunteering for programs to help change the status quo in developing countries or disadvantaged areas. Volunteering your help and skills in times of disaster is quite another matter. What is needed is an International Alliance of Relief Organizations to coordinate the efforts of all its members.

LOGISTIC PROBLEMS IN INTERNATIONAL DISASTER RELIEF SERVICES.

When a request for disaster help comes, many logistic problems arise. These problems become multiple when the request is international, especially when diplomatic relations between those countries are less than ideal.

To be effective in a disaster, time is of the essence and bureaucracy must be dispensed with while people are severely injured or dying.

We learned much in our response to Armenia's earthquake disaster of December 7, 1989, from Hurricane Hugo, from the Revolution in Rumania, from the 1990 Earthquake in Peru, from Hurricane Andrew and from numerous other emergencies and projects. These lessons need to be shared with others so that response in future disasters and projects can be more efficient.

In almost all situations, response to disaster should be through a group. An individual, no matter how well meaning, will find it almost impossible to get into a disaster area to help, except through an organization prepared to respond to such calamities. The exceptions to this are individuals who have very special skills and are asked by governments or organizations to consult with them.

Undoubtedly every group has problems unique to its own organization. Below are listed areas in which all organizations will find common problems.

1. COMMUNICATIONS

In today's world, the marvel of rapid communications is truly miraculous, providing all parties have compatible communications equipment. Incompatibility of equipment renders any high technology system virtually valueless. All organizations should strive to have compatible facsimile (FAX), computer, radio and telephone equipment. Of the above listed, FAX is perhaps the best communications tool we have today where the Internet is not available. It has amazed me how wide spread the use of FAX has become in the past few years. Even the most primitive of developing countries seem to have FAX equipment available today. When I was in Moscow in May of 1990 to present at a conference on disaster response, I remarked to one of my guides that it was good to see that <u>Glasnost</u> had freed up communications enough to allow FAX in the USSR. The guide looked about to make sure no one could hear, then sheepishly whispered in my ear, "Yes, but we can only receive messages, we are not yet allowed to send FAX out!"

If nothing more can be accomplished than to standardize communications equipment between countries, then we will have gone a long way toward providing the most efficient relief and disaster response system in history. Such a system should help get information regarding actual disaster conditions, and intelligence regarding needs and requests for specific response to those who can best provide aid in the shortest possible time. Such a system should avoid one of the most costly and wasteful problems in disaster relief, getting the wrong type of personnel and equipment into a disaster area at the wrong time.

Nothing is more frustrating or costly to a relief organization than to respond to a disaster only to discover their skills are premature or are being duplicated by other groups which could respond more efficiently and they are not needed at all. An adequate worldwide communications system should help coordinate multiple-organization efforts to assure their responses are needed and delivered in a timely manner and with proper priority sequence. It is also a serious problem that communications are often wiped out in the disaster area itself. If incoming aid organizations have satellite phones it can be tremendously helpful and life saving.

2. GETTING VOLUNTEERS

An efficient method of cataloging volunteers with their skills and ability to respond immediately after a disaster is essential. This can only be accomplished through organizations. A standby, on-call system must be established as well as a means of communications with these people. With this knowledge we will be able to inform any organization just how much of a response is needed from them, saving them the expense of over responding. If more of a response is needed than one organization can provide, the "Alliance" would be able to combine the response of two or more organizations to work together as a team, sharing the skills and equipment each can best provide.

In addition, the "Alliance" would be able to help member organizations recruit personnel with needed skills to round out their membership and enable them to deliver the most efficient relief and aid they can marshal.

3. PROVIDING FOR THE TEAM

Above all, a relief team must not become a burden to those it intends to help. Calamities usually create a problem in housing, feeding, transporting and communicating with the residents of the disaster area.

The disaster team must be as self-sufficient as possible so as not to take food and shelter from those it is trying to help. Equipment and food for each member of the team must be carried as efficiently as possible. Here again, an "Alliance" should be able to help its member organizations in determining what support equipment and supplies will be needed for the sustenance of the team in the field for their duration of service. In many instances the "Alliance" may be able to supply member teams with their sustaining supply needs.

4. GETTING MOBILIZED

Personnel and equipment must at times be packed and ready to go with essential documents, inoculations on a moment's notice. Here again communications is a key to efficient response.

As a coalition of organizations prepared for disaster relief, the "Alliance" would have sufficient stature and affiliation with the host country in which relief aid is needed, that they should be able to cut through diplomatic red tape for member organizations. They could keep current information regarding immunization requirements and endemic diseases the world over. This information would be communicated to member organizations immediately upon hearing of a disaster or request for assistance, and where possible the Alliance of Relief Organizations would help make immunizations available to volunteers.

5. GETTING THERE

It is unlikely that normally scheduled transportation will get personnel and equipment into a disaster area in the shortest possible time. Developing countries often have extremely poor transportation available, and these are the countries that tend to need the most help after disasters. Also, transportation expenses can be a prohibitive problem. Creativity and use of unusual methods are often the difference between success and failure. When our medical team from Doctors To The World had to get into Armenia quickly after the Armenia earthquake, Continental Airlines flew us to Miami from Denver (round trip) at no cost, and from Miami to Armenia we were flown (round trip) at no charge by an Armenian arms dealer, the only person who had cart blanch landing rights almost anywhere in the world. He was able to cut through government red tape that our State Department couldn't begin to help us with. Creativity in travel is essential.

In Viet Nam, during a Cyclone that flooded much of the country, Doctors To The World was able to get the Vietnamese army to transport us and our equipment to areas that were inundated in flood waters via amphibious vehicles.

The "Alliance" would solicit corporations who might provide private aircraft, trucks and other forms of transport in disaster and relief situations. Also they could maintain relationships with all commercial carriers and national airlines for help with transportation of member personnel and equipment during disaster events.

6. FINDING YOUR NICHE

Once the team arrives in the disaster or relief area, confusion, chaos, difficult communications, language problems, culture shock, transportation problems and inability to find leadership makes it difficult for the team to get started with its work. Initiative in finding the best place to work is often essential. However, an "Alliance" would be able to help its member organizations become situated and working as quickly as possible by setting up a communications and coordinating unit in the disaster area specifically to help organizations find where they will best be able to serve the people and host country. An "Alliance" could also be a communications service to member organizations and their home country, state or city. Where possible it could keep families at home informed of the situation and of the volunteers or their disaster and relief team activities.

7. FUNDING

Raising funds for non-governmental aid organizations, especially small groups, is becoming a constantly more difficult job.

As a coalition of relief and assistance organizations it would be easier to obtain grants, endowments, gifts, donations, corporate and government sponsorships which would be divided and shared among all membership organizations in an equitable manner. Furthermore, by letting an "Alliance" handle most of the logistic problems of member organizations, many of these tasks would not have to be duplicated by each organization, saving administrational costs and leaving more funds for the actual work of relief. Of course, member organizations would be free to raise their own funds in any manner and quantity they chose. Funds raised by the "Alliance" would be used for administration of the coalition and remaining funds would then be dispersed among member groups to help defray the costs of rendering disaster relief. It is extremely difficult for small aid organizations to compete with large organizations like the Red Cross who have national media connections to help them collect funding for disasters, though much of the aid work is done by these small groups.

8. REHABILITATION AND LONG TERM AID

Responding to a disaster on an emergency basis is a first priority, to minimize lives lost and reduce as much as possible any crippling and permanent injuries. However, once this is accomplished, it is important to return disaster victims to an active and productive life as quickly as possible. This might require long periods of rehabilitation, retraining and rebuilding. With a network of volunteers in all professions and walks of life and with a network of corporate and government connections it makes sense that an **Alliance of Relief Organizations** would take the next logical step and help establish and coordinate long term programs to help people and communities rehabilitate and get back on their feet.

An excellent example of this is Hurricane Katrina, which after two years is still trying to recover its losses. Government response to their needs has at best been a miserable and shameful failure.

9. LESSONS LEARNED

Our experience responding to Armenia's earthquake, Hurricane Hugo in the Caribbean, and Rumania's health problems after their uprising, as well as our long experience with aid to developing nations, has taught us many valuable lessons and has suggested these steps that can be taken internationally to help all disaster and relief teams to respond and work more efficiently in the future. It is important that we share these lessons and suggestions with others because in the case of international disaster relief and aid to the disadvantaged, efficiency means the difference between lives saved and lives lost. We at **Doctors To The World** hope all relief organizations will join us making an **Alliance of Relief Organizations** a real and viable tool to help all such teams respond effectively to any and all world disasters and areas of need and suffering.

Our experience shows that the only way to render disaster aid is through a closely coordinated effort by international disaster teams sponsored by organizations working in concert and joint venture. Over the years many of these small but effective groups have been forced into bankruptcy by larger organizations, especially the Red Cross, who have vast fund raising capacity but who have not shared the funds with the smaller groups who have put forth costly and efficient effort. Joint funding and coordinated effort is the only way for small non-government organizations to survive.

CHAPTER 11

YOU THE DIPLOMAT, GIVE OF YOURSELF

When you volunteer your services, be it on a mission to aid a developing country or in a team effort to assist in disaster relief, *you are a diplomat.* You are representing your country to the people and host nation you are abetting. You are the best type of ambassador to exemplify your country and its people. By the same token, *if you're a jerk, you can be the worst representation of what your country and its people stand for.* Please don't be a jerk! Fortunately, the great majority of volunteer types are resplendent individuals. Fortuitously, jerks don't tend to volunteer or give of themselves. Too bad the same can't be said for many of our career diplomats. The image of "the ugly American" is too real in many Third World countries.

Part of our career diplomats' problems is that they tend to live in diplomatic compounds and never mingle with the people of the host country. They live among themselves, entertain among themselves, go to school in private schools, mingle only with the high and mighty and look down on the people of the disadvantaged masses. You will be the counterbalance! Your work will be among the down trodden. Your brief time among those people can and will change the image of "the ugly American" to "the compassionate and giving American" in the minds of those who often resent us most.

So, how should you go about putting forth the best image of what your country truly is, what we stand for, who we really are?

Do not go with a superior attitude.

Your host country and its people may be disadvantaged, primitive, unworldly, simple, even childlike and naive in your eyes.

Remember, you are judging them by your standards. Their naivety may only be a sign of trust toward you. Mistreat them or in some other way lose that trust and they will seem naive no more.

Never let them feel you think yourself superior to them. You aren't. If you would judge superiority by the ability to survive in their environment with their resources, I think you would quickly find out who would be depending on whom for help. Remember your place. You are a professional and skilled person in one or two areas of expertise who has come to teach and serve in a special area of need. Serve up your help with care, kindness and in sincere friendship, and remember you are there to learn as much as you can from them, too.

Do mingle with the people.

You can't convince them you are a sincere friend if you don't rub elbows with them. If you're not socializing with them, you probably aren't a friend but just a specialist doing a job. If that's the case you are cheating yourself. But, if you get involved with them as people, take an interest in their lives and problems and joys, you will gain an experience you'll cherish a lifetime. If you go alone on a mission you are more likely to mingle with the folks. If you go as a group or with your family there is a greater danger of isolating yourselves.

If you take family, encourage your spouse and kids to get into the act. Seek out areas where your spouse can help. Persuade your children to play and interact with the local youths. Throw a party if you have to, for the kids and/or for the grownups. Locals may be shy and hesitant to "force themselves on you." They may feel it presumptuous to hope for a social relationship with you. Do not misinterpret that for surliness or cliquishness or unfriendliness on their part. Make it known from the beginning that you do not consider yourself above them and that you want to know them and to be their friends.

Do not go in with the idea of changing the world or even just the host area you'll be working in.

Too often we approach an underdeveloped area with the idea that we're going to Americanize them, jolt them into the twenty-first century, give them a taste of the good life, show them the true religion, "civilize" them, sell them our political system, save them from themselves. Which of the above should you try to accomplish? "None of the above," is the only correct answer!

All we should try to accomplish is make their life a little healthier, safer, easier. It is fine to let them know what we live like, but don't try to shove it down their throats. If you want to discuss your beliefs with them, fine, that's getting to know each other, but listen to their beliefs and don't try to convert them. Discussion of politics is alright, but don't enter their politics and don't argue yours. Discussion that is a two way street is O.K., usually, but in countries where there is a dictatorship, even a purely intellectual discussion of politics could land you in jail or at best get you expelled by their government. *It's best to stay out of political discussions.*

As for "civilizing" them; primitive does not necessarily mean they aren't civilized. Don't insult them by implying you are more civilized than they. After you get to know them better you may discover they can teach you a thing or two about civilization. After all, it probably wasn't their society that has been polluting our environment, raping the world resources, fighting wars all over the globe. I'll bet their crime rate is far lower than ours. Their religious leaders aren't stealing fortunes on TV like our evangelists. Child abuse, sexual abuse, drug abuse, hopelessness, even their infant mortality is probably not as high as ours here in the "civilized" U.S.A.

Your job is to help them, not necessarily change them.

Teach them what you can, but don't tell them what to do with the knowledge. That is their decision to make and they are infinitely more prepared to make it than you are.

Don't try to change their world, just make it a little better place for them.

If you are sincere in what you are doing, come in friendship, give of yourself, attach no conditions or strings to your service, and respect them, you'll be the best representative of our country and our people that we could possibly have on their soil.

CHAPTER 12

HOME SWEET HOME, RECRUIT OTHERS

No matter how wonderful and satisfying your mission might be, eventually it's a pleasure to come back home. If not, perhaps you should go back out on another mission. Part of that pleasure in homecoming is sharing your adventure with others. You'll be surprised in how much interest your experiences will arouse in others. The people who thought you were nuts to let yourself in for such an assignment will be first in line to "get the facts." Their, "I told you so," will wither into, "I wish I'd have gone." Well, that's your queue! "So go!" should be your answer to them. Lord knows there are plenty of places that need help and plenty of organizations needing personnel to send.

Your job now should be, after you pick your next assignment of course, to recruit others into volunteer service. No one can do it better than someone who's been there, and that someone is *you!*

To be well prepared for your job as recruiter of future volunteers you must also prepare before you leave. Become a multi media person. Carry slide camera, digital and/or film photo cameras, and if possible a mini video camera. You'll want no less for your own friend's and future enjoyment. When the word gets out that you're back, everyone will want you to present a slide show talk or a video talk about your exploit. You'll find yourself somewhat of a hero and celebrity and the envy of all. Schools will ask you to speak to classes. The organization that sent you may ask you to speak to new volunteers. Newspapers and T.V. interviewers will seek you out. It will all be a rather heady experience. The bottom line of each of your appearances should be, "You can do it too!" Let others know that they, like you, have something to give. If we could get everyone out there to give of their time, their talents, their skills, to give of themselves, just think how much better this world would be.

Ask the organization that sent you out to supply you with literature about their activities, and applications for potential volunteers. Pass them out at all your appearances, and to your acquaintances who you want to interest in serving. You might even be able to do some fund raising for them to help pay for your next mission.

More and more corporations are getting interested in encouraging their employees to do volunteer work. It's good business. It promotes good P.R. for the corporation and keeps employees from burning out. Your boss may want you to do a presentation for your fellow workers.

In some ways recruitment is almost as much fun as

having been out in the field. It surely helps you to savor the memories of your venture. And it is very satisfying in its own right to speak to interested audiences, especially school kids who are just developing value systems of their own. If you enjoyed making a difference in some developing country, take renewed pleasure in making a difference in the way some kids will think about helping their fellow men and women in the future. You will be a positive role model, something we have far too few of in our society today.

CHAPTER 13

STARTING YOUR OWN "PRIVATE VOLUNTEER ORGANIZATION" - (PVO)

When one thinks of volunteer organizations, one usually thinks of government organizations, church groups, huge civic agencies, religious associations or enormous international leagues. It will then surprise you to discover that most of the volunteer organizations making a huge impact all over this planet are small, non-government organizations (NGOs) or small Private Volunteer Organizations (PVOs), started by one or two or at best a few dedicated individuals no different than you and me.

I started **Doctors To The World** about three decades ago because I didn't like the way some of the organizations that had sent me out on missions operated. I found a few other physicians who felt the same, so we went out and found our own projects, got them funded and started doing our thing. As we got better and better at it we started getting requests from other areas of need. Word got out about what we were doing and more medical personnel joined our ranks. Today we have a pool of over 200 medical volunteers. When our dental ranks began to swell we spun off **Dentists For The World.** With time lots of non-medical people asked about what they could do. To answer their requests, **Doctors To The World** formed two sister groups, **Volunteers To The World** and **Student Volunteers To The World** for non-medical, teen, and college service minded individuals. We just kind of happened. We found our niche, filled it and grew in it.

If you can't find the ideal organization to satisfy your need to serve, then start your own. It is simpler than you think. After all, if you can recruit for someone else, you should be able to recruit for yourself. Be willing to start out small. Maybe you'll want to stay small. Here's how to go after it..

1. Decide on _your_ mission. What niche do you want to fill? What services or needs do you wish to address that some other organization isn't already filling or isn't fulfilling adequately?

Define your mission as precisely as possible. Focus. "I want to bring computer training to Central America." What ever it is, state it as succinctly and exactly as possibly.

2. Find some colleagues with the same passion. It is easier if you have some help. If your cause is worthwhile, you'll find lots of interest.

3. Incorporate. Form a not-for-profit corporation. You can do this yourself usually without the expensive aid of an attorney. You might find one who will do the work for nothing, as a contribution. Check with your Secretary of State to find out how to incorporate. It usually requires filling out a simple form and paying a few dollars. You may have to write a corporate statement defining your plans and purpose. Keep it as simple as possible.

That done, *you're a PVO and/or NGO.* You're **official.**

4. Apply for your 501(C)(3) certification from the Internal Revenue Department. This lets donations to your organization be tax deductible and your organization purchase your supplies tax free. Your success does not depend on this designation, but it helps and gives an air of legitimacy. Actually, many PVOs and NGOs are not tax exempt and do a fine, cost effective job. Your local IRS office has all the forms you need to apply for your 501(C)(3). If you can get an attorney or accountant to fill it out for you free as their service contribution, great! Or do it yourself. Keep it simple and follow instructions to the letter and you'll have no problem.

5. Look for funding. Money is the name of the game. You do not have to wait for your 501(C)(3) to be approved before you can solicit funds. If you go after corporate funding, it may be a business expense to them anyway and other tax exemption is not necessary.

Many corporations have foundations that give to charitable organizations. We prefer to go to their marketing people rather than their foundations. If I wanted to teach computer science to the people of Central America I'd go to the marketing department of IBM, Apple, or Dell and point out to them how my services will help them sell computers in Central America. That will probably get you funded quicker than asking a foundation for a grant.

6. Set up your project(s). Start out slow. Before you try to impact the world, dent a small community in Central America or in your own home town. This will give you a chance to shake out the wrinkles. It will also let you develop a formula that best works for you. Your formula won't fit every project, because every project will have some different problems, but it will give you a foundation program that will mold itself to most of your ventures.

7. Enlist your volunteers. Volunteers come from almost anywhere. If computerization of the Third World is your thing, colleges with computer programs, trade schools with computer programs, corporations using computer programmers, the general public with home computers, computer clubs, etc., are all sources for volunteers. Once the word is out about what you are doing the names will pour in. Announce your goals in church bulletins, company news letters, radio, TV and newspaper interviews and you'll soon be on your way. Develop a Web Page or get someone who knows

how to make one for you as a contribution.

8. Ally yourselves with other organizations traveling a parallel course. This may frustrate you a bit. Many organizations are so dedicated to protecting their own turf that they will have nothing to do with anyone who may horn in on their action. The bigger the organizations are, the more protective of their "empire" they seem to be. But keep looking. Soon you'll find some groups that are truly dedicated to their goals rather than to their own enhancement, and those are the ones you can start an alliance with. By sharing information, services, expenses and projects you will be able to work more cost effectively. Duplication of effort is a waste.

We at Doctors To The World learned early on that the best way to set up a program in another country was to try to find an orphanage, hospital or school in the host country we wanted to work in and see if we could operate through them.

This often gave us a place to work out of, and they were helpful in developing our relationships with the people and government officials.

9. Look for other goals and projects. You shouldn't spread yourself too thin, and you may not want to expand beyond your first goals, but from time to time you may recognize related areas where you can make an impact. Diversification isn't necessarily bad. With time needs change, people burn out, interests wane.

Diversification might bring new life blood to a stagnating organization. Think about it.

10. Always remember your goals. Be satisfied to make your impact however small. Don't try to change the world. If you just make it a little healthier, safer, easier, or friendlier you've made it a little better place for all of us to live in.

What more could anyone ask of you?

APPENDIX I:

Following are described a few of the volunteer programs Doctors To The World has been involved in. They are included here to give you an idea of the different types of programs that are available and their differing levels of ease or hardship and difficulty.

MEDICAL MISSION, HONDURAS August 6, 1983

Othniel J. Seiden, MD

A few weeks ago I'd have said, "There's little adventure left in this world, and certainly none for me," I can now attest it would have been a misstatement. Even when I volunteered to go to Honduras for the Victoria and Albert Gildred Foundation for Latin American Health and Education, I couldn't have suspected it would take me to jungle villages where no medical doctor had ever been before ... or to refugee camps where Miskito Indians, victims of Nicaragua's

Sandinista government suffer a new type of political extortion at the hands of the United Nations service teams known as AGNUR. Least of all could I have dreamed I'd spend time with the leaders of "MIZURA," a major group of "Contras" made up of Miskito, Zumo and Rama Indians. The name Mizura is made up from the first two letters of each tribe name ... Mi Zu Ra.

Like the majority of North Americans, I hardly knew where Honduras was, much less anything of its people, problems or economy. I had an inkling that President Reagan was sending troops to the area for some kind of military maneuvers, and wondered if there wasn't some better way he could spend my tax dollars. I was certainly confused about the role of Honduras in the Central American wars that involve Nicaragua and El Salvador. My experiences enduring three weeks of giving medical services to the refugees on the Honduras-Nicaragua border have done much to change my philosophy on giving U.S. aid to foreign nations, and has left me with a thorough understanding of what the wars in Central America are all about.

The Victoria and Albert Gildred Foundation has sent many physicians and educators to areas all through Latin America, but this was the first request they'd received from the Miskito Indians in Honduras. They got my name through another organization with which I've registered for volunteer medical service, Direct Relief International. I got a phone call from the director of the Gildred Foundation, Mr. John Fisher of Miami, Florida during the last week of July, '83.

"Would you be interested in doing a tour for us in Honduras starting August 6th? I know it's short notice, but...."

Well I guess it was meant to be, because when I looked at my schedule book, doubting that I'd be able to do it on such short notice, it worked out that the three weeks he wanted were about the only ones relatively free of things I couldn't change. "Let me make a few phone calls and get back to you. If I can change a few appointments, I'll do it." It all worked out and I agreed to go, and then discovered my passport had expired by three months. More phone calls. I must give credit where credit is due. If most government offices are inefficient bureaucracies I can't say that the Passport Office is. As soon as they realized there was an emergency situation, I was able to get my new document from San Francisco to Denver in just two days.

My first foreign night was spent in the Maya Hotel in Tegucigalpa, the capital city of Honduras. It is a fine hotel, and the only hint that this was to be an unusual stay was the obvious invasion of CBS, NBC, and ABC video news people. They were there to cover US troop maneuvers. I had no idea I would be in any way concerned with any of this.

Let me enter a note here. The names I use from here on are fictitious unless I state otherwise. The reason for this is that many of the refugees I dealt with, either as patients or those who helped me get into the villages where patients were to be seen, still have relatives in Nicaragua. Many are in Sandinista prisons or are in positions of jeopardy. Not knowing who might read this report I do not want repercussions to befall anyone, especially those refugees who make trips back into Nicaragua from time to time and at great risk.

That first evening in Tegucigalpa I was met by Mr. Wycliffe Diago (his real name), Coordinator of Health for the Miskito Indian Refugees. He and three other Miskitos struggled through the language barrier with me (I speak only English, German and some Yiddish). Thanks to what powers there be the Miskito Indians are trilingual, and almost all speak broken English, Spanish and Miskito. They explained to me that I'd be picked up early the next morning, 8:00 am, and taken to an airfield to begin my adventure into the refugee camps.

Let me enter another brief note here. If an American (U.S.) comes to Central America, he should throw away his watch. Time is not an exact science there. The people are content to sit and wait. I'll admit they are far less stressed; in fact I wonder if they know the meaning of the word stress. Anyway, at 9:37 I was on my way.

When the Gildred Foundation sent me to Honduras, it was to go to the UN Camps set up to take care of about 30,000 refugees from Nicaragua. I was under the impression that that was where we were going.

As we drove through the city in a four-door Toyota truck with a camper shell on its bed, I was informed that we were going to drive to another city, San Pedro, and catch the plane there. I never really understood the explanation of why, but thought little about it at the time. The drive was beautiful even if the road through the Honduran mountains was less than ideal. They asked a lot about me, my country, why I came there, what I knew about the refugee problems, and how I felt about the wars in Central America. We talked about President Reagan, how happy they were that he was sending troops to Honduras for military maneuvers and how they hoped it would slow Castro's and Russia's influence in Central America. In retrospect, I realize now that they were finding out all they could about my philosophy, feelings, motives, etc. They were subtle, friendly, clever, and after five hours on the road to San Pedro they knew a lot more about me than I knew about them.

I guess they liked what they found out about me because as we approached San Pedro they asked me if I'd be willing to go into their small Miskito Indian villages and see where a real medical need existed. They explained that the AGNUR people treated patients only in the official United Nations Refugee Camps and that there were thousands of refugees in the little villages in remote areas where the UN teams refused to go to.

I agreed to go under two conditions; that what I was going to do could not be in any way construed as a political involvement by the organizations I represented, and that I was exercising my own judgment and would have to have supplies furnished since I had neither medications nor tools of my trade. We struck our agreement.

There was a great deal of conversation among my companions in what I thought was Spanish and couldn't understand. Later I was to find out it was Miskito which I also couldn't understand. After some minutes Wycliffe Diago, whom I shall refer to as Cliff from now on, informed me that one of the others in the truck knew of a pharmaceutical firm in San Pedro that might be willing to give us some medications. We stopped off at the plant, a large building and indeed they gave us two large cases filled with broad spectrum antibiotics, antihistamines, vitamins, cough medications, anti-fungus ointments, gastrointestinal medications, aspirin and numerous other things I thought we might need. They virtually filled my entire list of medications and supplies I'd asked for which was a great surprise to me.

As we drove past the San Pedro airport they informed me we would be going on by truck to the city of La Ceiba since I had agreed not to go to the UN refugee camps. It was another five hours over even worse roads to that Atlantic Coast city. It had been a very long day. We drove to a large home where we seem to have been expected. We were fed and there I met several new persons, including a man who looked to be in his early thirties, Stedman Fargot (his real name).

The table conversation repeated much of the questioning of the morning's truck ride. It appeared Mr. Fargot was satisfying himself that I was who and what I claimed to be, a physician from the United States who was willing to give three weeks of my time and talents to a tribe of Indians I'd never heard of before. I explained to him that although the Gildred Foundation did not pay for my services, they did cover all my travel expenses so that what I was doing wasn't such a big deal. I guess my conversation satisfied him, too. He told me to get a good night's sleep, that tomorrow I'd be flown to a remote town on the Atlantic Coast about thirty miles from the Nicaragua and Honduras border.

The next morning as we drove past the entrance to the La Ceiba International Airport. I guess Fargot noticed the surprised expression on my face, because he laughed and said, "No, we aren't going to drive ten hours today." He explained that there were no roads to Puerto Lempira, our destination, but that we were not going to fly commercially. We only drove about a kilometer past the airport and turned into a Honduran Military Base. After a long dialogue in Spanish that my companions held with the military personnel, I found myself getting into a Military DC3, vintage 1941.

First the plane was loaded with a large amount of crated supplies, then I was loaded on and told to sit on a bench along the inside of the plane, kind of like paratroopers in a World War II movie. There were no seat belts. I was given a length of rope and told to tie myself to one of the struts along the body of the plane. Soon we took off and as I looked over my shoulder and out a window I noticed we were skirting the treetops, clearing them by little more than fifty feet. Strange, I thought. We flew like that for a little over forty-five minutes and then landed in a narrow clearing in the jungle. The plane bounced along to a stop at one end of the clearing and made a quick 180 degree turn about. The door was opened and the crates of supplies were off loaded and then I too was ushered out of the plane. No sooner had my feet touched the ground than the aircraft gunned its engines, which were never stopped, and the DC 3 took off, leaving me, the supplies, Cliff and Fargot standing in the clearing. As soon as the plane cleared the trees at the end of the clearing, about thirty uniformed armed men came out of the jungle and headed straight for the supplies. With unbelievable speed and efficiency the supplies disappeared into the jungle forest as if carried off by a column of ants. Cliff, Fargot and I followed them. I didn't know it at the moment, but I'd just been joined by the Contra forces.

Puerto Lempira is a quaint town of about 800 Miskito Indians. There are no phones and no electricity unless you have a generator, and I saw only three places that did. Running water is rare and flush toilets are unknown. The place I stayed at did have flushing type toilets, but to use them you had to draw a bucket of water from a well and when you were through, the water had to be poured into the bowl. It was a step in the right direction!

The last thing I was told as the sun was setting, "Be up at 7:00 am and we will load onto trucks to drive to the nearest villages south of here."

"How long a trip is it?" I asked.

"About three or four hours."

At 5:00 am a knock came at the door to my room. "Get up! We have a change of plans. A boat is going to another village and it leaves in just a few minutes!"

It took me five minutes to shake off the sleep, get dressed and throw my things together. I learned quickly that I shouldn't unpack but take out of my bag only what I'd need when I needed it. I was at the dock at 5:10 am. I waited as they loaded the boat with supplies - food, medications, those we picked up in San Pedro as well as others, and instruments that the Honduran military had given us. By 6:00 am I was in a 30 foot boat about 6 feet wide. It looked to me like an old dugout with an old inboard engine. They started bailing water out of it it within minutes after we left the dock.

They'd picked a windy day for the trip and waves were higher than the boat. We traveled down the Atlantic coast toward Nicaragua, about a half mile off shore, keeping the coastline barely in view. For twelve hours we bobbed over and through the waves. More frequently than I liked, waves broke over the boat and the men bailed constantly to keep up. I was drenched the whole time, thankful that the ocean water was warm. Three times during the day we were overrun by squalls. The rain was cold and piercing, driven by strong wind, feeling like needles against my skin. Worst of all was the sunburn. I ended up molting for the next ten days.

At about 5:00 pm we reached the Coco River, the border between Honduras and Nicaragua. They saw the concern on my face as we turned up it. "Don't worry, we control that area of Nicaragua," one of the

Miskitos assured me. However, they hugged the Honduran edge of the river and broke out weapons for each of the "crew." We continued up the Coco for the better part of an hour. Just before dusk, which is at about 6:00 pm in Honduras the year around, we turned into a narrow tributary on the Honduran bank and were met by two Indians in a dugout canoe. They escorted us up that tributary for about a half mile and there was Eliah, a Miskito Indian village.

It was like stepping back in time. I felt I should be doing an article for *National Geographic Magazine*. Thatch roofed huts on tall stilts first caught my eye. At the same time, I had caught the eyes of the natives. Gringos are not a common sight in that part of the world. My companions announced that I was an American doctor come to help them with their medical needs. I could see awe on their faces, but I couldn't fully appreciate it. I was exhausted from exposure on the sea and to the sun, thirsty, and I think a little feverish. Coming to this place as night was falling just added to the culture shock. I waded ashore on wobbly legs. They took all my luggage and supplies. Throughout my journey they never let me carry my own things. There was a constant desire to help me all they could.

We walked through the village to the biggest of the huts and turned in. "This is where you stay while you are here," I was informed. I was to stay with a family, in their home, and in their care for all my needs. I climbed the ladder up to my room, a dark small space with a "bed" in one corner, the only furniture in the tiny space. The bed turned out to be a cowhide stretched over a wooden frame. Hard? It was like sleeping on a drum head. But I was so exhausted it didn't matter.

There was no electricity in the village. I didn't know what I wanted to do first; get out of my wet clothes, take a long drink or collapse. To tell the truth, I felt miserable. I was afraid to drink the water, but one of the Indians who had accompanied me brought me some water and assured me it had been treated. Thirst won me over and I drank, and drank. I took off my clothes and was surprised how sore my muscles were. I got into some dry swim trunks, put insect repellent on my exposed torso and remember nothing more until the roosters crowed the next morning. It was just dawning. I peered out at my watch. It was 4:30 am. That is dawn the year around in Honduras. In the semidarkness I saw three people sleeping on the floor next to my bed. The family had shifted around their sleeping arrangements to make room for me in the best bed in the house, the only bed. Later that day I told them that I felt bad that I was causing them such trouble. They assured me that it was an honor to have "the American doctor" stay with them and that they insisted on the arrangement.

After breakfast which consisted of red beans and rice and very strong coffee, I set out to take my first real look at the village. It was much less a culture shock in the daytime. The first thing I noticed was a lot of uniformed, armed young men - "Contras!" The Contras are anti-Sandinista rebels who are backed by the Honduran and U.S. Military. Most are Nicaraguan refugees who are carrying on a fierce struggle against the self appointed Communist Government in Nicaragua.

I cannot discuss the number of Contras in the Miskito villages, but Eliah had over a thousand residents without counting the Contras. In addition, there were several hundred non-combatant Miskito refugees who had been taken in by the villagers. It was those people I had come to treat.

At this point in time I had little opinion as to the politics involving Central America. I wanted to reach these areas where medical help was needed, and the Contras were the only group who could get me there.

One of the Contras who spoke exceptionally good English took me to the medical hut. It was not as nice as the place I'd been given to be 'my home away from home.' He introduced me to another Contra who was their medical officer. He spoke poor English. My interpreter told me he had been a medical student in Nicaragua prior to the Sandinista takeover. He was in his last year of studies when he was arrested and escaped. He'd been in Honduras since 1980. Together we made rounds and house calls, throughout the entire village. I treated some forty people that day, teaching as much as I could to the "corpsman" who would have to maintain the "practice" after I left.

He was a very talented young man and I learned a few things from him about insect bites, funguses common to the area, and local remedies for certain illnesses. He, of course, had much more experience with malaria than I. One boy we saw had fallen out of a coconut tree the day before and fractured both forearms. The Contra had splinted both arms quite expertly. Of course we had no plaster to cast the arms so there was little more that I could contribute. I'm quite sure the boy did well under the care of this young Contra. He and I had long discussions through our interpreter and I was able to answer many questions that he had.

Most of what I saw in that village over the next three days were fevers of unknown origin with weakness and fatigue. I suspect that parasites are the cause for much of this problem. One of the biggest frustrations there was the lack of even the most basic of diagnostic lab equipment.

Other problems, and these were prevalent throughout the many villages I traveled, were fungus disease of the skin, nausea and vomiting, diarrhea, cataracts, and scarred sclera of the eyes. Much of this was inflicted by Sandinista torture, as were the torn out fingernails, scarred backs and feet, crushed hands and severed tendons. Boils and pustules of the skin were fairly common and urinary infections were also. I doubt that the urinary problems were venereal or TB. The Genito-Urinary problems responded to treatment with sulfa and pushing of fluids, and I was able to show the medical officer how to lance some of the pustules in an aseptic manner when they were ready.

Trauma was not too frequent a problem. Malnutrition and dehydration was seen only when I stayed in a United Nations refugee camp about which

I'll go into more detail later. Malaria was a problem, but mainly among those Miskitos who came out of Nicaragua.

On the first day that I was in Eliah, a girl of about twelve was brought to me in a hammock slung from a long pole and carried on the shoulders of two Contras. She had a history of not being able to walk due to severe thigh pain upon bearing weight. Examination disclosed a large tumor erupting through the skin. I had no X-ray, of course, but the mass went deep and felt adherent to the bone. My fear was that this was a bone cancer and I told the Contras that she needed immediate hospital care. They made arrangements to boat her to Puerto Lempira. From there the Honduran military flew her to La Ceba, and a modern medical facility. Of all the problems I saw in the three weeks, the worst were those caused by torture inflicted by the Sandinistas - more about that later.

Overall the Miskito Indians are a hardy bunch with relatively little illness considering the conditions under which they have had to live over the past few years. They are a meticulously clean people. Their teeth especially were in excellent shape and I saw them constantly cleaning them, three and four times daily or more. They bathed at least once a day in whatever water was available. The only time I noticed any body odor was on myself after I had to hike twelve miles in ninety plus degree, humid heat and that was remedied by a plunge in a fast stream along with my companions.

It was while I was in this village, Eliah, that I found out that Stedman Fargot was the top man in Mizura, leader of this Contra movement since its beginning. My time in Honduras would be closely linked with him for the duration, for without him and his Contras I could not have moved about to accomplish what I did. I must emphasize again that I had not been brought here to give medical aid to the Contras, but was being made available to the refugees by the Contras.

After three days in this area, Fargot, four armed Contras and I started back to Puerto Lempira, this time in a faster boat, a twenty foot fiber glass outboard. It took us only eight hours this time, even though we stopped at three other villages along the way. I can't go into the locations of these villages for security reasons. The villages were smaller and health problems were far less than in Eliah.

It was after dark when we returned to Puerto Lempira, and that night I slept on a floor in a warehouse with a sack of rice as a pillow. I was too tired to mind the hardness of the floor, but when I realized that I was surrounded by roaches I wasn't too happy. An idea struck me that fortunately worked. I sprayed a line around my blanket with insect repellent. They didn't cross, for which I was most thankful!

The next morning we left by truck for some of the U.N. refugee camps. The first we stopped at was Tapanlaya. It was a small camp, desolate and depressing. There was no medical facility there. It was the first place in which I saw malnutrition and dehydration. Intermittent fever, lethargy and weakness were the most common symptoms. Compared to the camps I had seen before, this one was the most depressing. I could understand why these people preferred to stay in the villages of their own people rather than in the U.N. camps. I did what little I could there and then we went on to the main U.N. refugee camp at Mocoron.

Mocoron was enormous in comparison. Two-thousand refugees still lived there, although it had been reduced from nearly twenty-thousand. There was an airfield and the major AGNUR medical clinic. We drove directly into the camp and I moved in with the refugees. The same illnesses prevailed there, but again I saw malnutrition, dehydration, and for some reason, a higher incidence of urinary infection with flank tenderness and dysuria. Pushing fluids and Sulfa tablets seemed to do the trick. This was the standard treatment in their clinic.

When I asked about their diet I was told that AGNUR, five letters that stand for five Spanish words meaning United Nations High Commission for Refugees, allowed each refugee 3 lbs. of red beans, 1 1/2 lbs. rice and 1/2 pound of flour per week. In the Contra camps the ration was considerably more supplemented with small quantities of meat and fruits and vegetables that are brought back from raids into Nicaragua. To make matters worse, the refugees reported that if the AGNUR people suspected that any member of a family is a member of the Contra, the U.N. would cut off food supply to the family. To me, this seems a form of political extortion. The Miskito Indians consider the U.N. people as very leftist and I saw no evidence to argue the point.

While in Mocoron I saw about sixty patients. I asked them why they didn't go to the AGNUR clinic and they told me the doctors treated everything the same, with one aspirin tablet. I don't know how true that was, but I never found anything else they told me to be untrue. I saw several people who had been labeled as having TB by AGNUR. When I asked them what tests had been run on them to make the diagnosis they answered, "None!"

Finally I decided to go up to the clinic to see it for myself. I tried to ask questions of the staff, but all claimed they spoke no English. The Indians told me they do speak English. I saw about five nurses, a couple of lab technicians and no doctor. I seriously doubt that no one could speak English.

In Mocoron, I had a chance to talk to many of the refugees about conditions under the Sandinistas. They told me of arrests without giving a reason or trial, of genocide, of people disappearing. They spoke of torture and showed me fingernails that had been torn out, hands that had been crushed, scarred backs from whippings and scarred bottoms of feet from the same treatment. Many had tendons that had been cut. A favorite of the Sandinistas was to cut Achilles tendons and sever tendons in the wrists that made the thumbs and forefingers useless on the dominant hand. Many of the refugees had scarring of the sclera of the eyes. They told me that a common torture was to throw pepper and sand in the eyes while hands were tied to chairs.

In the two days that I lived among the refugees in Mocoron I never saw anyone from the AGNUR medical or administrative staff enter the refugee area. I feel it unfair to criticize AGNUR too severely without their having a chance to explain their side of the story but I certainly feel a thorough investigation of their administrative, medical and political practices would be in order.

From Mocoron we continued south toward the Nicaraguan border. I was settled into a thatch roof structure with open walls in the main camp of the Mizura Contras. This would be my base camp until I was ready to return home. This base, known as C.I.M.M., was a military encampment and training center for the Contra. Again I was not there to treat military personnel but would live there and would hike into numerous refugee camps throughout the area to treat those Miskito Indians who refused to go to the U.N. camps. AGNUR refused to give any food or medical care to these people and it is here the need is greatest.

One of the saddest sights in the military camp was to see boys between nine and fourteen in cut down uniforms. I was told that these children actually go into Nicaragua on raids and that those in this area had all been in at least two times, and most upward of six times. All had seen action and carried weapons. I asked Fargot what kids like these could understand of war and the answer was simple and to the point. He said, "We call them 'wortoguya,' the littlest ones. They know that if they point their rifle accurately a Sandinista will die and if enough Sandinistas die, then maybe one day their father or mother or brother or sister might come out of prison alive."

All along the border on the Honduras side there were villages built by the Contras and Miskito Indians of Honduras to house refugees from Nicaragua. Several hundred people live in each of these settlements. Food is obtained for them by the Contras and the Miskito Indians of Honduras. They eat better than the refugees in the U.N. camps. They have a larger allotment of rice and beans, some fish and meats and fruit and vegetables that the Contras bring over from their raids into Nicaragua. I ate with these people as well as those in the U.N. camps and the food was more varied and more plentiful.

The types of illnesses were the same as I had seen in other areas but there was none of the malnutrition that I saw in the U.N. camps. Again there were "medics," and a few exiled Nicaraguan nurses to help me. In fact among the refugees in the camp at Mocoron I met the first nurse ever graduated in Nicaragua. She had retired after 43 years of work and was pressed back into duty in the camps. I spent many hours with these medical people answering their questions, teaching them what I could about continuing care and left with them some medications that they could use in continuing care.

Upon return to Puerto Lempira on my way back out, I had a long discussion with Cliff. I explained to him that it was really impractical to have physicians travel from one village to another as I did. As interesting as the experience was it was not an efficient way to bring medical care to the Miskito Indians of Honduras or the refugees. I felt it was necessary that I saw their conditions and needs but it would be better to have a central clinic where modern lab and diagnostic facilities could be established, and where a physician could work far more effectively. Puerto Lempira would be an almost ideal location for such a medical facility. It is within a few hours of almost all the villages I visited, and patients could be easily transported in by truck or boat. Two outboard motor boats could get patients in from the coastal villages and trucks could transport pateints from those places located to the south and inland.

The Miskito Indians suggested that they could build the structure if physicians and supplies could be sent in. I recommended the idea to the Victoria and Albert Gildred Foundation and they felt it a viable idea. Hopefully, in the near future there will be established in Puerto Lempira, the Victoria and Albert Gildred Foundation Atlantic Coast Clinic for Central America. I would love to be the first volunteer physician to man it.

###

As a result of the above volunteer mission, Dr. Seiden was called to Washington D.C. to testify before congress. Often volunteer missions have far reaching affect and can give you a positive impact in the world situation.

Tegucigalpa 06229.

State Department unclassified telegram,

State Department official complains about the UNHCR's double standard for its refugee camps in Honduras, which, he explains, involves applying the concept of a refugee being treated unevenly as to people fleeing from El Salvador and those fleeing from Nicaragua.

Thus some UNHCR personnel reportedly refuse to believe that there even is a possibility that their camps could house refugees from a leftist government. Wycliffe Diego, former Coordinator of Health for the Miskito Indian refugees, and himself a Miskito Indian, told The Heritage Foundation that UNHCR employees and refugees should be removed from the frontier and potential military sites in order to provide security and protection for the refugees.

Dr. Othniel J. Seiden, an American physician sent to Honduras by the Victoria and Albert Gildred Foundation in August 1983 reports that U.N. teams have refused to offer medical treatment in many of Nicaragua's Miskito villages. He also writes that the refugees told him that, if the U.N. staffers suspect any family member of being a member of the Contras (anti-Sandinista rebels) the U.N. cuts off food supplies to the entire family. States Dr. Seiden, "To me this seems a form of political extortion. The Miskito Indians consider the U.N. people as very leftist and I saw no evidence to argue the point." Indeed, State Department officials catalogue decidedly leftist biases not only on the part of UNHCR employees but also-particularly their contractors or partners." The principal operating partners in Honduras are World Relief, the Honduran Red Cross, Caritas Honduras, the Mennonite Church, Catholic Relief Services, Medicines sans frontiers, and Comitk

Evang6lico de Desarrolo Nacional (CEDEN).13 Other voluntary agencies that cooperate with UNHCR MOUNTING UNHCR PROBLEMS The UNHCR is probably one of 'the least politicized United Nations agencies. Its humanitarian work has been praised by Jeane Kirkpatrick, Permanent Representative of the U.S. to the U.N and others. The Nobel Peace Prize extended to the office of UNHCR in 1954 and again in 1981 was in all likelihood well deserved. The agency, however, has not been free of criticism. The refugee camps "continue to be politicized, with pro-Sandinista posters and slogans." The UNHCR uses terrorist national liberation movements as contractors for Southern African refugees in Angola.

Othniel J. Seiden, M.D Medical Mission to Honduras," paper delivered at White House Outreach Conference, June 27, 1984

###

Doctors To The World still has a program in Honduras in Zona Miskito. However it is not as high a level of hardship as it was during the Contra war. For more information on the Honduras program today contact Louis Perrinjaquet, MD, Doc P-J, at **<docpj7@gmail.com>**

APPENDIX II:

For other programs Doctors To the World has been involved in over the past decades, and to show you the variety of volunteer opportunities available, the following is taken from a past DTTW newsletter.

DOCTORS TO THE WORLD - DENTISTS FOR THE WORLD
   HEALTH USA -
      VOLUNTEERS TO THE WORLD & STUDENT VOLUNTEERS
         NEWSLETTER

Doctors To The World to narrow its scope and widen its world!

Future **Doctors To The World** *projects will, with few exceptions, work with and through orphanages and homes for homeless children.*

If we can make an impact with the needy children of a developing country or underserved area, we can have far reaching effect for decades to follow. Though we may be narrowing our scope a bit, we will broaden our areas of functioning.

We will be able to get to work quicker, with less investment, more cost effectively and in many more areas of the world. By working through existing honest and well functioning host organizations. In the host country, we will have an immediate home base to grow from as well as an infrastructure to utilize.

In addition we will have a ready made team within the country to help us with logistics, transportation, and translation, people who know the local customs and political ropes, who can help our volunteers to get established at work and to help them feel a part of the community.

Furthermore, increasing emphasis will be placed on **Volunteers To The World** *and* **Student Volunteers To The World.** *This will help include physicians' and dentists' families in our projects and will allow non-medical projects to be included for lay volunteer work. Our work will still be apolitical and without religious obligation.*

Volunteer Vacations *will be emphasized to allow people to perform satisfying, benevolent, fulfilling work while enjoying various cultures, adventures and experiences. Since the purpose of* **Volunteer Vacations** *is to bring aid, to the needy, all expenses of the* **Volunteer Vacation** *should be tax deductible under Doctors To The World's (501)(C)(3) IRS status. Participants should check with their Tax Advisors.* **Volunteer Vacations** *will arrange all air and land transportation, guides and translators where needed.*

Volunteer Vacations *will take on three major forms; work sabbaticals, dialogue sabbaticals, and combination sabbaticals:*

Work Sabbaticals *will emphasize hands on work with the people in need.*

Dialogue Sabbaticals *will emphasize fact finding and problem solving tours of the host country or area. These will often be first time forays into an area to set up a program.*

Combination Sabbaticals *will evolve both fact finding dialogues and hands on work with the people to solve their problems.*

A listing of future **Volunteer Vacations** *will soon be available.*

For further information or input for the development of specific programs you would like to see contracted, please e-mail to dttw@juno.com

DTTW Projects:
Medical Programs.
Barbuda

Caribbean Island - 30 miles north of Antigua - 1200 residents - English speaking - DTTW once ran the only medical facility on the Island - 4 nurses and staffed with volunteer doctors year around — minimum tour is one month. Excellent snorkeling, wind surfing, fishing, bird watching (165 varieties and one of the only 3 Frigate bird rookeries in the world, hiking, exploring, archeology, 206 known ship wrecks off shore — three bedroom three bath house -vehicle - great duty - wife and kids will love it! Need dentists, physicians.

Nevis

Caribbean Island near St. Kitts - 14,000 residents English speaking - has five doctors on the island - DTTW sends periodic specialist help and periodic generalists to fill in when local doctors are off island. Also can use nurse practitioners, PAs, technicians, etc. Beaches, boating, fishing, exploring, scuba, flora. Minimum duty one or two weeks but will try to work a four week tour to be split up among several other islands.

Saba

Caribbean Island - 60 miles south of St. Martin - Dutch but English speaking - Has one general practitioner full time. DTTW sends periodic specialty help and occasional generalists when doctor is off island. Fifth best scuba area in the world (deep cliff diving), fishing, boating, flora, exploring, mountainous, no beaches but one of the most scenic spots on earth. Need dentists.

Dominica

Caribbean Island - 94,000 population - English speaking - has many doctors - DTTW sends specialty help and generalists when local doctors are off island. Beaches, fishing, boating, exploring, flora, mountainous and rain forest, bird watching, Photography.

Anguilla

Caribbean Island - 5 miles north of St. Martin - 7,000 population - English speaking - has five doctors - DTTW sends periodic specialty help and occasional generalists to fill in for local physicians when they are off island. Also need Nurses, nurse practitioners, Pas, EMTs, technicians, physical therapists, pharmacists, psychiatrists, etc. - Spectacular beaches, fishing, boating, bird watching, and hop over to St. Martin.

Eastern Europe

A new program which will send physicians to Russia, hopefully by summer 1995, is now being put into place. Physicians who are willing to go for at least a month, to teach Russian physicians new techniques in almost all areas of medicine. This will be a continuing program. The Eastern Europe experience is for the whole family.

Israel

We have made a joint venture with _Dental Volunteers To Israel_ and are sending dentists to their Children's Clinic in Jerusalem. We will also send them hygienists. Our first volunteer left October1st, 1993 and would like to send at least a month. We hope to have our dental program expanded one to several small communities, offering service to youths from 5 to 18. Projects will include Ethiopians, Russians, Bedouins, Druze and all other needy Israeli children. We are also recruiting volunteer doctors and nurses who can help with Health education. Minimum service one month. Families are encouraged to accompany volunteers.

Santo Domingo

New program to work with orphans and "Cave children," homeless kids who live in caves along the coast. Joint venture with **Cry Of The Caribbean** who feed these kids and give many a home. Need pediatricians and generalists, specialists, nurses, PAs, nurse practitioners, EMTs, dentists, educators, help of all types.

Honduras

Reestablishing program to Zona Miskito. Most primitive spot on earth. Only adventurers need apply. Living in jungle Indian villages. No plumbing. No roads. Some generator electricity. No phones. Malaria. True third world experience. Need generalists, nurses, nurse practitioners, PAs, dentists, EMTs. Minimum duty two weeks to 1 month. Probably not for the kids but O.K. for an adventurous spouse.

Vera Cruz, Mexico

An exciting new Volunteers To The World Program! For Doctors, Dentists, Students, Nurses, Volunteers from all walks of life is located in Gutierrez Zamora, VERACRUZ, Mexico, a city and district near the eastern or Caribbean coast. This will be an ongoing program much like Barbuda, with volunteers and their families rotating through on a continuing basis. Gtz. Zamora has a state run hospital which needs help with equipment and medical personnel, but our volunteers will be rotating through government clinics in the barrios and villages surrounding Zamora. Doctors will work 4 to 5 hours 4 days a week giving ample time to enjoy the beaches, culture and people of the area. It is an ideal area to take the family. And if they want to volunteer their services, even your teen agars, there will be plenty for them to do. And you will all learn Spanish as if by osmosis. If you speak no Spanish you will be provided with a translator.

Volunteers and their families will be staying in Tecalutla, a small tourist village on the coast, at the Hotel Tecalutla, a fine beach front facility with air conditioning, clean Caribbean beach, beautiful pool, excellent restaurant and service. Electricity is 110 in most places. A splendid full meal with drinks will range in the $5 to $8, i.e. fillet of beef or fish or sea food (poultry is cheaper) perfectly prepared. The town itself is a seaside resort town with shopping and numerous quaint restaurants all within a few blocks walk. Crime is negligible in the entire area. Many of the tourists in the area are from Canada and Europe, further broadening the cultural experience for you and especially your kids. Reliable sitters are available for your young ones.

Air fare to the area is in the $500 to $500 range. R.V. Camps are available in the area. All expenses should be tax deductible7

There are many archeological sights in the area, temples, pyramids, ancient villages, and the area is steeped in history and tradition. People are friendly, clean, hard working and family oriented. The major religion of the area is Catholicism. Fishing is fantastic and inexpensive.

Horse back riding is available and inexpensive. Boating readily available on rivers and sea an inexpensive. Bird watching is spectacular. Temperature ranges between 72 to 85 the year around and there is a cool prevailing breeze of the sea most of the time. You can go for as little as a week, or two, or three, or as long as you want. We expect this program to fill up quickly, but we can also use several volunteers at the same time. **Ideal SVTTW program.**

Ecuador

DTTW was involved with successful eye program that replaced 100 cataracts with intraocular lenses, treated numerous other eye diseases and squints. Plan reestablishment of more permanent ongoing programs in future.

Belize

DTTW has been requested to develop ongoing clinic program.

Rumania

DTTW was in Rumania immediately after start of revolution and aided Rumanian orphans by arranging non-medical volunteers to help care for those neglected children. DTTW plans for Rumania to be included in future continuing Eastern European programs.

Armenia

DTTW provided one of the two American medical teams who went into Armenia immediately after their devastating earthquake in 1988. DTTW plans for Armenia to be included in future continuing Eastern European programs.

San Miguel

DTTW has been requested to develop ongoing clinic program.

Nepal

DTTW has been requested to develop ongoing clinic program. Emphasis will be on pediatrics. Will need physicians, dentists, nurses, nurse practitioners, PAs, EMTs, technicians, etc. DTTW is helping to recruit physicians for a clinic in Katmandu, Nepal. Volunteer will have to cover airfare, but housing expenses in Nepal are covered.

Haiti

DTTW has been requested to develop ongoing clinic program. Emphasis will be on pediatrics and general care. Will need physicians, dentists, EMTs, nurses, nurse practitioners, PAs, technicians, etc. Also need volunteers in many other professions and fields. Waiting for political situation to cool down.

Vietnam

DTTW is recruiting doctors, nurses, technicians, health workers of all type for ongoing programs. Dr Sheldon Kupper, a dentist left for Vietnam (Oct 17, 1993) to set up our <u>Dentists For The World</u> dental program there. We will be furnishing two complete dental facilities in Danang. Presently we are working with <u>Volunteer Eye</u>

<u>*Surgeons International*</u> *to establish an ongoing ophthalmology program. All of our projects are in the Danang area where we are running an orphanage taking care of about 30 children. Also, we're working with several schools for the handicapped and have given over a hundred scholarships to keep children in the poor mountain areas in school through high school.*

Peru

DTTW will try to help a small clinic with volunteers in Iquitos, Peru for Dr. Linnea Smith, who is the only medical care available to the Indians of this extremely primitive but fascinating and beautiful part of the rain forest world.

Doctors To The USA - Rural Health Projects - Children's Outreach America....

Charity begins at home. As the health care crisis deepens here in the USA more and more requests have come to DTTW to plug our developing country assistance formulas into our own health care systems. We've responded to the request by first targeting the problems of rural America. It has become our most ambitious and important project.

Purpose:

Find suitable physicians, PAs, nurse practitioners to provide good medical care for rural areas otherwise deprived of full time local physicians.

Provide medical help for rural physicians who are overworked or need specialty backup.

Provide medical care for the <u>medically indigent</u> of the area, <u>especially children</u>.

Their transportation, housing and local car rental costs will be covered by the program so the physician or other volunteer will only be giving his or her time. The program also provides that the volunteer will not have to work more than a thirty hour week, giving plenty of free time to enjoy the small town experience and the activities the area offers. The experience will also give the "city folks" a chance to see if rural medicine might be for them.

If you are interested in serving for a three week **Volunteer Vacation** on a 78 foot two masted ketch that was once the yatch of the King of Spain, sleeping eight and with a crew of three in the West Indies next fall call dttw@juno.com, ASAP. Four comfortable double cabins, all meals, snorkeling, sailing, fishing, comradery ... a wonderful volunteer vacation adventure. Interested in a **Volunteer Vacation** to Cuba next spring? Ten days fact finding trip offering CME and nursing CE credits. Will tour the entire country to determine needs for future DTTW projects. Or, CME and CE fact finding trip to Dominican Republic next spring to work with our affiliate orphanage, Cry of the Caribbean and determine further needs in the surrounding barrios.

If any of these Volunteer Vacations interest e-mail to receive further information as soon as it becomes available!

(This ship has since been sunk in port during a hurricane.)

What is Doctors To The World?

DOCTORS TO THE WORLD is a charitable, service organization qualified and recognized by the United States government with tax deductible status, 501 (C)(3), dedicated to aiding the underprivileged, here and abroad, with health science services, education, as well as economic and environmental *improvement.*

MEDICAL SERVICES *of Doctors To The World bring volunteer medical personnel ... physicians, nurses, technical and support people ... into areas of vital need, in the United States or the world over in a maximum cost effective way. DTTW was one of the two medical disaster teams to work in Armenia immediately after the December, 1988 earthquake. DTTW was also involved in relief efforts during and after hurricanes Hugo in 1989, Andrew in 1992 and in Missouri during the summer floods of 1993 ... and was in Rumania during their revolution in January 1990. We went to Peru after that 1990 earthquake. Locally DTTW is launching a program, HEALTH USA, to bring medical services to the growing population of American medically indigent. DTTW also sends volunteers into clinics in the West Indies, Netherlands Antilles and works in Central and South America, Vietnam, Israel.*

EDUCATION *services of DTTW include an active speaker's bureau making information available to schools, groups, industry and developing countries. DTTW brings volunteer educators, technical and skilled persons into underprivileged areas to help the people develop knowledge and talent to improve and maintain a better lifestyle.* **DTTW STREET SMART** *program, a highly successful tutorial program for Denver inner city grade and high school youths, was* **the recipient of one of President Bush's 1,000 Points of Light awards.**

DISPLACED PERSONS *services of DTTW works with refugees in foreign lands, such as the Miskito Indians in Honduras as well as homeless street people in our own cities. DTTW offers these displaced people medical services, food, clothing, shelter, aid in obtaining gainful work and help to reenter productive society.*

CLEAN INDOOR AIR COALITION (CIAC) is a branch of DTTW dedicated to educating people about the major indoor air pollutant injuring our health, side stream tobacco smoke. Through CIAC, Doctors To The World sponsors QUIT SMOKING NOW! a smoking cessation program available to the public, industry ... and offered to public schools at no cost. You can help in the continuing efforts of Doctors To The World by volunteering your time and talents and by sending your tax deductible contributions to:

Doctors To The World dttw@juno.com

Why Volunteer?

Free international travel and adventure! Doctors To The World, a charitable service organization needs volunteer members from all areas of expertise: Physicians, Dentists, Nurses, Paramedics, Laboratory techs, Farmers, Carpenters, Plumbers, Educators, Engineers, Entrepreneurs, Social workers, Government employees, Technicians all types, Home economists, Business people, Retired folks ... anyone with skills, trade or profession. If you can travel a few days or a few years to help others, we can use your skills. To more efficiently accomplish our agenda, **Doctors To The World** *has established two new divisions.* **Dentists For The World** *to serve dental needs throughout the world, and* **Volunteers To The World** *for non-medical needs both in the United states and the World. Both* **Doctors To The World** *and* **Dentists For The World** *are made up of volunteers from the medical community; physicians, dentists, nurses, nurse practitioners, paramedics, emergency medical technicians, physical therapists, PAs, Medical and nursing students, x-ray and lab technicians, medical equipment maintenance people, LPNs, medical administrators, etc.* **Volunteers To The World** *is made up of volunteers from all other walks of life; Farmers, Carpenters, Plumbers, Educators, Engineers, Entrepreneurs, Social* workers, Government employees, Technicians all types, Home economists, Business people, Retired folks - anyone with skills, trade or profession willing to impart his/her talents and knowledge to the underprivileged or developing areas of the USA and world. **Volunteers To The World** will help in areas where construction, education, logistic support, introduction of more efficient methods, planning and other assistance are needed. **VTTW will play an important part in our efforts here in the US to benefit the homeless.**

Also, we have established a subgroup of **Volunteers To The World , Students To The World.** It is our strong belief that the best time to learn one's own worth is during the teen years, and we feel there is no better way to learn about one's own merit than to share knowledge and talents with others. When teenagers do worthwhile volunteer work they gain far more than they give. They also set a positive course for themselves that will serve them well throughout their entire future. **STTW will also be heavily involved with homeless projects here in the US.** Both VTTW and STTW will also work on our international projects.

These organizations work extremely cost effectively because our volunteers donate their time and talents. Usually the host country or community provides housing and area transportation for the volunteers. We hold the work to a level so there is plenty of time for the volunteers to explore and enjoy the area where they are contributing. In cases where the host country or community cannot supply adequate housing and area transportation, we seek other sources of contribution.

In addition to volunteers, we are always seeking **corporate partners** in our projects. We say "corporate partners" in that we are not asking for a hand out. We generally approach the marketing department of a potential corporate partner who will benefit from its affiliation with our project. We can offer a corporate partner a foot in the door to an area where they want to establish their products or business. They can gain tremendous **public relations** *benefits by supporting our work and do some real good while they are at it. Our philosophy is not to get just one corporate sponsor to bear all the costs of a project, but to find many non-competitive companies who can benefit from affiliation at a modest cost. Corporations can affiliate with as many projects as will benefit them.*

Doctors To The World (DTTW), Dentists For The World, Volunteers To The World (VTTW) *and* **Students To The World** *are not turf protectors as too many other organizations seem to be. We welcome working with other service organizations. It is very cost effective if we don't always have to reinvent the wheel. If another organization with similar goals has already laid some ground work, we will be happy to join in their effort and save us both time, effort and expense. Likewise, if we've already made inroads toward a common goal, we will gladly let other groups join in with us. We welcome the help. Our bottom line is to bring relief to the needy in the best and most efficient manner possible and usually cooperation will benefit all.*

At present we have a **pool of over 2,000 volunteers.** *Most are in the medical fields ... the majority are physicians.* **We want more! More physicians, more dentists, more nurses, technicians, students -** <u>**more folks just like you!**</u> *Please give us your time, your skills and talents. Become a volunteer family. You'll never regret it!*

Remember, all donations to Doctors To The World are fully tax deductible. *We need financial help as well as man/woman power. Please be generous with your donation of funds, too. Our work is very cost effective and every penny of your donations will benefit those less fortunate.* <u>Doctors To The World has no payroll.</u> <u>Everyone works as a volunteer. Every penny is spent on our projects.</u> *Donations should be made out to:* **Doctors To The World** *and should be sent to:* **Doctors To The World**
P.O. Box 37167

Denver, Colorado 80237

An **Application form is in this newsletter.** *Please fill it out and send it to the above address. Join with the most wonderful people on this earth and become a volunteer. This world has a lot of problems. By volunteering you can become part of the solution. Feel free to make copies of this newsletter and the application and give them out to interested friends. That too is a form of volunteering.*

Residency Programs

DTTW has been asked by several residency programs to design a project for Third World or local need locations. We are delighted to work with any residency or med school student program.

Doctors To The World *assisted in:*
Armenia Earthquake, *one of only two American medical teams to participate.*
Hurricane Hugo, *on Barbuda and fund raising for North Carolina.*
Peru Earthquake, *working with Ministry of Health to avert epidemic and evaluate rehabilitation needs.*
Hurricane Andrew, *providing volunteers to work in Homestead, Florida in the* **Humana Free Medical Care Clinic.** *An average of 100 and upward storm victims were seen each day.*
Missouri Flood, *immunization and treatment of minor trauma in Jefferson City, MO.*

Dear patron:

As you can see **Doctors To The World** *is going through a tremendous growth process, both with starting its new divisions,* **Dentists For The World, Volunteers To The World, Student Volunteers To The World, Health USA,** *and* taking on **new programs here in the USA and throughout the world.** *As you know, growth requires increased funding. Since Doctors To The World is neither a religious nor a government organization, such funding comes mainly from individuals who are willing to share their good fortune with those less blessed with prosperity.*

There are two ways you can share your good fortune with those who are underprivileged. One is by volunteering your time and talents in an area of the US or the world where your skills will make an impact and a positive influence on peoples lives. Secondly you can help fund our programs with your tax deductible donations to Doctors To The World. **If you can't give a few weeks of your time and talent volunteering in the field this year, give one day at your job for us. That's 1/365th of your income as a donation to our programs.**

Please give generously of both your skills and other resources. Thank you!

Update on Vietnam 8-22-94

Since October, 1992, when Dr. Seiden and Mr. Dzung Anh Do traveled to Vietnam to determine first hand the progress of DTTW projects and to evaluate other program needs. DTTW and DFTW have had an active presence there, and DTTW has had personnel working in Vietnam since October of 1992.

In Danang, our orphanage is home to about 30 children. DTTW hopes to place these children in loving homes both in and outside Vietnam where they will have opportunity to reach their potential in education and life.

In QuangTri Province we've established over 100 scholarships for students who show promise for college work. The scholarships will allow those students to finish their secondary education and qualify for college entrance.

DTTW is working to establish clinics with outreach programs into the surrounding provinces. These clinics will be staffed with our volunteer physicians, dentists, PAs. Nurse Practitioners and Lab personnel and will interface with the local Vietnamese medical community to help deliver medical care to the needy populations. Volunteers will go to Vietnam for a minimum of four weeks, and will get exposure to the north, middle and south of the country. Ample time will be available for touring and exploring areas of interest.

Vietnam is one of the most beautiful countries in which DTTW has been involved and the people are extremely friendly toward Americans. Prices for food, lodging and souvenirs are still very low everywhere. Vietnam has about 72,000,000 people, one third the population of the United States, all crowded into an area the size of New Mexico. We started our volunteer program in Vietnam in October of 1993, as planned, with the volunteer Dental services of Dr. Sheldon Kupper. If you're interested let us know now when you might want to go.

Yes, I'm interested in participating in Doctors To The World - Dentists For the World - Volunteers To The World - Student Volunteers To The World and Health USA Programs.

Name_____

Address_____

City,   **State,**   **Zip**
_____

Phones H_____
W_____
FAX_____
My profession, occupation or area of expertise is:

_____
_____

Please send this form to: Doctors To The World
P.O. Box 37167
Denver, Colorado 80237

CUSTOMIZED TRIPS TO ISRAEL

Bargain Rates — Often Tax Deductible — Group Flexibility

Special trips to Israel, customized to the interests of your group, profession, church, synagogue, organization, etc. Any length trip that fits your needs. Variable price from budget to deluxe. Likely to be tax deductible! Fund raising potential for your organization. Maximum flexibility to provide you with the trip you want at the price you can best afford. Seminars in virtually any subjects for your group's interest. Programs take you to sites throughout the country relating to your interests, led by experts on your topics of concern. All costs of air fare, programs, housing, some meals and touring covered in one low price. Special air and land rates. You get the best possible tour of Israel at the lowest possible price and with tax advantages as well. Ideal for church, synagogue, mosque groups, all religious groups, student programs, medical, dental, professional, retirement groups of all types. Duration can be from one week to a full year program. We design your seminar program to fit your specific needs and interests. **Sponsored by Israeli Government Education Program, the College For National Studies and Doctors To The World,** *a charitable volunteer organization.* **All proceeds go to charity.**

A few seminar topics:

Medicine topics — Dentistry topics — Public health topics — History of Israel — Hebrew — Yiddish, a living language — Military history topics — Agricultural programs — The Church in Israel — The Arab in Israel — The Palestinian and Israel —

Economics of Israel — Archeology of Israel — Mossad, Shin Bet and security in Israel — Kibbutz programs — Student programs, high

school, college, post graduate ... credit possible. — Volunteer programs for students, adults, seniors.

If you have a group with a special interest listed above or want a program even more unique, contact Doctors To The World —-
Doctors To The World -P.O. Box 37167 — Denver, CO 80237. Or dttw@juno.com

REVIEW DTTW Agenda & Projects:
Medical Programs.

Barbuda	*Nevis*
Saba	*Dominica*
Anguilla	*Eastern Europe*
Israel	*Honduras*
Ecuador	*Belize*
Rumania	*Armenia*
San Miguel	*Nepal*
Vietnam	*Haiti*
Santo Domingo	*Doctors To The USA*
Rural Health Projects	

Children's Outreach America.
Rural USA
Health Education

Disaster Relief. *Jefferson City, MO, Missouri River Flood 1993*
Armenia - Rumania - Peru - Honduras - Hurricane Hugo - Hurricane Andreew - QuangTri, Vietnam Typhoon

11.
Organization.
Board of Directors

Othniel J. Seiden, MD
John Griffin
Dr. Nic Sol
Carl Erickson
Howard Newmark, DDS
Advisory Boards
Othniel J. Seiden, MD - USA
Amos Harari, MD - Netherlands
General Yigdal Danon, MD - Israel
Dr. P. Dias, MD, MPH - Nevis, W.I.
Dr. Levon Kostandian - Yerevan, Armenia
Dr. Boris S Sheiman - Ministry Health Ukraine
Gyorgy Vidacs, Ph.D. - Hungary
Howard Newmark, DDS
Dr. Irma Newmark, PhD

Please keep in mind that this is a news letter from 1995 and is only to show you an example of the type and variety of programs which might be available to volunteers. Today DTTW has programs only in Mexico, Honduras and Nepal. For further information on the Honduras and Nepal programs contact

Louis Perrinjaquet, MD, at <docpj7@gmail.com>

For Mexico programs contact
Mary Bacre, dttwmex <mbacre@hotmail.com>
or
Anna Tseng <ann_g_tseng@yahoo.com >

###

APPENDIX III:

Questions one should try to find out before initiating a volunteer program or intending to work in a developing or foreign country:

Volunteers To The World New Project Information Sheet

1. Location?

2. Needs of the area?

3. Languages spoken?

4. Religions of the area?

5. Other organizations working in the area? Will they be cooperative? What specific projects are they working on? Are they interested in joint venture?

6. Government officials we'll need to clear with, i.e.; Ministry of health, education, interior, etc.

7. Contacts you have made: names, titles, addresses, phones, FAXes, E-mail. How contacted? What was the gist of your communications?

8. Are there foreseeable oppositions to volunteer efforts and what might they be?

9. Are there local efforts to fill the needs of the area? What are they?

10. What facilities are available for our volunteers to use? (Housing, work areas, clinics, hospitals, labs, transportation, rental cars, equipment, tools, local materials, medications, class rooms, community buildings, etc.)

11. Who do we have to clear with to begin working? (Licensing, permission?
What are the local professionals working in the area who may see us as threat or competition; doctors, dentists, a medicine chief, teachers, priests? Do they understand that we would be there to help them and not take food from their table? Do they want us? Is it understood that we would only see the people the local professionals can not help or would not help?

12. What is the political picture? Is the area safe for volunteers? Is there high crime in the area? Are there endemic health problems? What are they? Would they be a danger to our volunteers?

13. Is there adequate healthy food available for our volunteers?

14. What are housing and food prices like? Local

resorts, apartments, RV facilities, cabins, restaurants, etc.

15. What recreational facilities are in the area?

16. What are points of interest in the area?

17. Are the locals friendly to outsiders?

18. Do the locals want us?

19. What is your personal impression of this location and its needs as a worthwhile program for Volunteers To The World, Student Volunteers To The World, Doctors To The World or Dentists For The World?

20. Further comments:

Appendix IV

If you are interested in testing yourself as a volunteer, to see if the volunteer experience will be rewarding and pleasing to you, try some close to home volunteer opportunities. Check out one or more of the following:

Local hospitals always need volunteer help in their gift shops, at their library carts, in delivering messages to patients, to cheering patients who have few visitors, to man reception and information desks and phones, to transport patients from department to department and many other important jobs. Many hospitals use teen volunteers as well as the elderly.

Local schools need volunteers as hall and playground monitors as well as street crossing guards. Often they use office help from volunteers. Tutoring is often a volunteer opportunity in schools and can be extremely satisfying.

Libraries often use volunteers in numerous capacities. Call you local library and inquire as to what volunteer positions they may have.

Hospice volunteers are a very special group of people who give aid and comfort to their patients and families in the last weeks and days of life. Contact a local hospice near you and inquire about what volunteer needs they have, or check out the book, *"The*

Hospice Experience" by Othniel Seiden, MD & Jane L. Bilett, PhD, www.boomerbookseries.com, through Thornton Publishing, or Amazon.com.

Your Police Department may use volunteers for any number of jobs, some even using volunteers to ride with officers cruising their beats. They usually offer extensive training for their volunteers.

Live theater and concert halls often use volunteers as ushers and other help, usually rewarding their volunteers by letting them enjoy free viewing of plays and concerts.

Churches, synagogues and mosques usually are a great source for volunteer opportunities. They will surely welcome your inquiry and help you find your best volunteer match.

Museums, art galleries, zoos, botanic gardens and other such places need volunteers for their gift shops, libraries, as ushers for special showings, as guides and any number of other positions. A simple phone call will get you on your way.

Boy and Girl Scouts will welcome your inquiry to volunteer for them.

The American Cancer Society, American Heart Association, The American Diabetic Association and almost all associations tied to any disease need volunteers for their programs to survive. Pick any one and call.

Check with your local court system who may use volunteers to help guide children and youths at risk or have other volunteer opportunities.

These are but a few organizations that you can pick

from to begin your life as a volunteer. As some of your friends and acquaintances that have already joined the millions who are already volunteering their time and talents. They'll tell you there are few greater joys than the Joy of Volunteering!

APPENDIX V:

Dr. Othniel Seiden, MD is available for training lectures to any corporations or organizations wanting to send volunteers or employees into foreign or developing countries.

Contact through **dttw@juno.com**

This book is available at a discount to any organization or corporation ordering more than five copies through www.BoomerBookSeries.com.

More From Othniel

Health

5 HTP The Serotonin Connection:
*The Natural Supplement that helps
you be in control of your mind and body!*
ISBN: 1519148445

5-HTP and Depression Management:
Available in Kindle Only

5HTP and Memory Loss Management with:
Available in Kindle Only

5 HTP PMS and Menopause:
Available in Kindle Only

Coping with Arthritis:
ISBN: 151941353X

Coping with BPH:
*Benign Prostatic Hypertrophy
Male, over 45, you probably have it!*
Available in Kindle Only

Coping with Colorectal Cancer:
*Prevention and Cure of theSecond Leading
Cause of Cancer Deaths*
Available in Kindle Only

Coping with Fibromyalgia:
It's not in your head, it's a disease!
ISBN: 1519438311

Coping with Prostate Cancer:
Prevention and Cure
of Man's Most Common Cancer
ISBN: 1519438737

Heart of a Woman:
Prevetion and Cure of the #1 Killer in Women
ISBN: 1519441533

Heavy and Healthy:
Forget Your Weight and Get Fit!
ISBN: 1519495412

Quit Smoking Now!:
The Program to Help You
Quit Smoking Now and Forever!
ISBN: 1519495781

Sharpening the Aging Mind:
Methods, Tricks & Tips to
Keep Your Mind Super Sharp
ISBN: 1519496028

Sleep Disorders Management:
Available in Kindle Only

The Second half begins at 50:
Your Longevity Handbook
ISBN: 1519496389

Walk!:
Walk Your Way to Great Health & Long Life
Available in Kindle Only

Weight & Appetite Management:
Available in Kindle Only

Relationships:

Adultery Case Histories:
> *Why People Cheat on Their Partners*
>> **Available in Kindle Only**

Communing with the Dead:
> *Death Needn't Part You*
>> **ISBN: 1519190085**

Foreplay:
> *The True Focus of Great Sex*
>> **ISBN: 1519440979**

Sex in the Golden Years:
> *The Best Sex Ever, Stay Sexually Active for Life*
>> **ISBN: 1519495927**

The Big O:
> *Male & Female Multiple Orgasms*
>> **ISBN: 1519496109**

The Hospice Experience:
> *Making Your Most Important Final Decision*
>> **ISBN: 1519496281**

When Your Spouse Dies:
> *A widow's & widower's handbook*
>> **ISBN: 151949646X**

Jewish Fiction

Padre Pio:
> *The Capuchin – the life of Padre Pio -*
> *St. Pio of Pietrelcina*
> *Sex, Horror & Violence vs. Unyielding Faith!*
>> **ISBN: 1519495684**

Seed of Avraham:
A 4000 Year History of the Jewish Family...
ISBN: 1519495811

Shtetl:
The Story of a Life No More...
As told from the hereafter
ISBN: 1519496036

The Cartographer:
1492
ISBN: 151949615X

The Condemned Voyage:
The S.S. St. Louis - 1939
Available in Kindle Only

The Crusades:
The Jewish World of the 12th Century
Available in Kindle Only

The Death of Berlin:
A Story of Hollocaust Survival and Revenge
Available in Kindle Only

The Remnant:
The Jewish Resistance in WWII
ISBN: 1519496346

The Uprising of Babi Yar:
The Syrets Deathcamp
Available in Kindle Only

Miscellaneous

Guaranteed Routes to Success for Writers:
A Road Map Through Today's
Dramatic Changes in Publishing
Available in Kindle Only

Joy of Volunteering:
Working and Surviving in Developing Countries
ISBN: 1519495587

So You Want to Write a Book:
ISBN: 1519496079

IF YOU LIKED

The Joy of Volunteering

PLEASE LEAVE A REVIEW ON
AMAZON.COM

ALSO AVAILABLE IN KINDLE